THE MACMILLAN SHAKESPEARE
ADVISORY EDITOR: PHILIP BROCKBANK,
Professor of English, University of York

GENERAL EDITOR: PETER HOLLINDALE,
Senior Lecturer in English and Education,
University of York

THE MERCHANT OF VENICE

THE MACMILLAN SHAKESPEARE

THE MERCHANT OF VENICE

Edited by

Christopher Parry

M

Macmillan Education

First published 1976
Reprinted 1976, 1977, 1978, 1979

Published by
MACMILLAN EDUCATION LTD
Houndmills Basingstoke Hampshire RG21 2XS
and London

Associated companies in Delhi Dublin
Hong Kong Johnnesbury Lagos Melbourne
New York Singapore and Tokyo

Printed in Hong Kong

This edition is for
MARIANNE ISABELLE
with love

CONTENTS

INTRODUCTION

'*The Merchant of Venice* is a great play, let us make no mistake about that. Alas, that it has been staled and hackneyed for so many readers by the treadmill methods of the classroom. . . .' So says John Dover Wilson in his book *Shakespeare's Happy Comedies*, and his sentiments are good and true. It is only right to add, however, that the determination of critics and teachers to interpret the play as a 'happy' comedy – when it is, rather, a caustic and saddening one – has done much to stale it; and nothing has hackneyed it more in schools than too rigid an insistence on *reading* the text, when it is meant, obviously, to be performed. As strongly as any of Shakespeare's plays, this one calls for acting.

NOTIONS

Whether or not suitable 'drama facilities' exist where the play is studied in school, a performance of it can, and always should, be arranged in the theatre of the mind. And any considered performance, even the most rudimentary, is likely to start sabotaging some of the notions that some classroom treadmills have sustained. The notion that this play is a fairy tale is one such. Another is the notion that it has two main plots – a romantic one, involving lovers and caskets, and a villainous one, involving ducats and a pound of flesh. A third is the notion that Shakespeare himself is 'on the Christians' side'.

The Merchant of Venice is no fairy tale. In a performance of it we do not find ourselves in a fantasy world, charmingly distanced from our everyday one by a frame of 'Once upon a time . . .' and '. . . happily ever after'. We find instead, at every turn, the accents and attitudes of our own consumer society. Today conventional notions of Success and Romance are as firmly bound to money, to ruthlessness and risk, as ever they were in the first Elizabethan age. Rather than a fairy tale, the play may be called a parable – that is, a fiction that calls us to consider critically men's behaviour in some representative moral situation. As a fiction it is certainly closer in kind to *The Prodigal Son* than it is to *Jack and the Beanstalk*.

The notion that there are two main plots (converging in the trial in Act Four) has arisen, no doubt, because there are two settings – Venice and Belmont. But the things that are set there – the art of dealing with the Jew, and the business of wooing Portia; the bond for flesh, and bonds of love – are related factors in one continuous process of exposure (of which the tale of Lorenzo and Jessica is a part). In this one process the play is all about the way powers of judgement are affected by the spirit of a venture. It is concerned with three main kinds of human bondage – amorous, filial and legal – and all three are clearly introduced in Act One. All three are explored in Venice and Belmont alike as the play proceeds. (It is worth noting that these two locations have characteristics in common. Belmont is not merely a romantic setting for Portia; it is a place where business is conducted, where accounts are rendered, where scores are settled. Venice is not merely a commercial setting for Shylock and Antonio; it is a place where true love is sworn and wondrous virtue celebrated.)

As for the play's Christians, Shakespeare no more forgives them their trespasses than they forgive Shylock, who trespasses against them. Not one of them practises the mercy that Portia preaches. And the final 'harmony' at Belmont does nothing to redeem the moral outrage per-

petrated in court at Venice. The play arouses aversion and
sympathy for the villain Jew and sets these feelings against
our sympathy and aversion for the prodigal Christians; and
in this way Shakespeare holds up the scales for his audience.

A MATTER OF BALANCE . . .

If, in the great trial scene, Shylock were simply foiled and
then sent packing without his principal, we might watch
the proceedings in comfort, even with relief. As it is, however 'right' Bellario-Portia's interpretation of the law may
be, it offends common sense, and we are shocked when the
foiled Shylock is crushed by cool, calculating, Christian
judgement. It is pointless to argue that Antonio's Christian-
ising 'mercy' will give Shylock's soul a chance of eternal joy.
There is no mercy in an enforced conversion; and nobody
in the play gives a damn for Shylock's soul (with the excep-
tion of Gratiano – and he gives his damn literally). When
the Duke of Venice threatens to cancel his reprieve of Shylock's life unless the Jew obeys Antonio's orders, the quality
of mercy *is* strained, out of all recognition. It becomes, to
put it mildly, the quality of bullying: 'He shall do this, or
else. . . .' The so-called favours that Antonio shows are all
deep and direct losses to Shylock, and they so huddle on his
back at this point that, in effect, they bury him alive. The
outcome plainly demonstrates that 'if a Jew wrong a
Christian' the latter's humility is indeed revenge, since the
conditions that Antonio imposes on Shylock are harsher
than the sentence previously pronounced.

Such judgement-with-a-vengeance is painful to watch.
It hurts our notions of true Justice and of Christian charity
(unless those notions are very superficial and complacent
ones). Yet there is also pleasure. a certain, semi-sadistic,

3

satisfaction, a sense of 'poetic justice', to be found in this outcome. However 'wrong' his sentence may seem to us, Shylock is a murderous, implacable villain. After bullying his victim with some relish (in III. 3), he comes to the court as a taunting tyrant. He says he craves the law, but he plainly means to kill. To him the words 'justice', 'judgement' and 'the law' all mean, simply, a bloody vengeance. When the vengeance strikes nearest his own heart, he gets strictly what he has been asking for; and the irony in this, the just-ness of the sudden turnabout, gives a certain pleasure; for it is always satisfying to see the biter bit. (Shylock is repeatedly presented in the play as a biter, a dangerous, snarling creature of prey: 'I'll go in hate to feed upon / The prodigal Christian . . .', 'Since I am a dog beware my fangs . . .'. His desires indeed are 'wolvish, bloody, starved, and ravenous'. The bond itself is a way of biting at Antonio. And the trial brings the passions of the Bear Garden into the Globe. The unedifying spectacle of Gratiano's baiting tactics, however, should keep our own feelings from running to excess.)

. . . AND OF DUAL RESPONSES

Although bloodshed is avoided in Act Four, neither Jew nor Christian emerges from it with any great credit, and in the overthrow of Shylock the audience responds with contrary feelings in quick succession – with satisfaction and dismay, with pleasure and pain. The climax of the trial is the play's most intense demonstration of the double-edged technique through which the vulnerability of bonds and the frailty of human trust are repeatedly exposed. Act Five, for instance, brings the message home in another key. The sublime diversion of the romantic Belmont night – with its lovers in the garden, its moonlight, its music and its contrivance of harmony (momentarily punctured by a presumably drunken Gobbo and by an image that powerfully recalls Shylock to mind: 'The man that hath no music in himself . . .') – all this gives way in the dawn to the farcical discomfiture of husbands and the deliberate contriving of discord laced with bawdy. The quarrel over the rings is both an amusing romp and a pointed warning, for the ladies' double game has implications both humorous and serious. Basically it teaches Bassanio to get his priorities right, to put his new marriage above every other love – which is something he had not learned to do in Venice. There, when he gave away his ring at Antonio's persuasion, he betrayed a bond that he had sworn in absolute terms to Portia. In doing so he put more trust in his love for Antonio than in his love for his wife; and Portia, by play-acting the scolding wanton so painfully well, shows him that she will not stand for it. Her charade puts Bassanio's relationship with Antonio firmly in its place. For the audience, of course, the episode is chiefly a comic entertainment. We know that Portia's vehemence is largely simulated, because – as luck would have it – her ring has remained in her own keeping. But an ominous note lingers under the comedy of this pantomime all the same – it shows us how awesome Portia *could* be, and it reminds us of the outrage that was all but committed in Venice when the trial was over.

To the assembled company Portia dispenses benefits at the end of the play, but just how *forgiving* she is towards Bassanio is nowhere made explicit in the script, though most directors give him the benefit of the doubt. He is only saved from disgrace by the amazing piece of luck that Portia and Lawyer Balthasar were one and the same person. And Antonio is saved from poverty by quite incredible luck:

'. . . three of your argosies / Are richly come to harbour suddenly.' Such fortunate chances do not make for an altogether comforting ending. We are more likely to leave the play feeling 'how lucky these people are to be getting away with it' than 'how right that it should all work out like this'. In other words, the play may be aiming to make us critically alert, rather than contented, because – like two-headed Janus – it looks at life in two ways at once.

FORTUNE AND THE TRICKY WORLD

The double-edged tactic can be seen in the treatment of the idea of Fortune – an idea in which the dual meanings of 'destiny' and 'money' frequently fuse together in the play. It is Portia's fortune to be 'richly left', for instance, and Shylock's to be a usurer. On one view Fortune works in a conventional way as a chancy force beyond human prediction, both kind and cruel in dispensing its surprises to mortals: it unites Portia and Bassanio in love and wealth, and it wrecks Antonio's ventures almost simultaneously. But on another view Fortune appears as a force of human ingenuity. There is nothing supra-human about the Fortune of Lorenzo and Jessica when they elope together: they help themselves to it, through some cool planning, with results both kind and cruel. Their romantic venture brings them happiness (and wealth) while it brings pain and rage to Shylock.

When the play's two leading figures, Portia and Shylock, encounter each other in a trial of strength, they act, in a sense, as agents of Fortune, she representing its possible love for human life, he its possible hatred. (He is, after all, the inheritor of an ancient grudge issuing from centuries of racial–religious oppression; and, as Coleridge put it in a nutshell, 'the oppressed will be vindictive'.) The court proceedings can then be seen as a kind of testing-place where the worst that Fortune may bring against a man (through Shylock) is tried (out) in the face of the best it may do for him (through Portia). What is 'decided' then is not simply the fate of Antonio but whether Fortune is, ultimately, friend or foe to Man. If the trial seems to prove that in the last resort Fortune's powers are more life-upholding than life-denying, that proof is – as has already been indicated – disturbingly shaky. It saves the play from turning into tragedy without making it into happy comedy.

In Portia's performance in court, Fortune plays its chief trick: 'This bond doth give thee here no jot of blood; / The words expressly are "a pound of flesh" . . .' – and it is a breathtaking piece of bluff (since flesh contains blood by definition), the *pièce de résistance* in a play that is full of tricks great and small. From the early moment when Bassanio says to Antonio 'I urge this childhood proof / Because what follows is pure innocence . . .', we watch truth being disguised in one way or another in almost every scene. Sometimes this is literally a matter of dressing-up (as the contents of the caskets are dressed up in gold, silver and lead, for instance; as the masquers dress up in suits of mirth and Jessica dresses as a boy). Sometimes the trick lies in putting on a deceptive tone of voice (as Shylock does in wooing Antonio to agree to his bond; as Launcelot Gobbo does to bewilder his old father; as Portia does in the closing scene to teach her husband a lesson). When Portia turns herself into Lawyer Balthasar she exploits both these kinds of disguise.

The play's world is characteristically tricky, and those people who 'get on' in it are those like Antonio and Shylock who, seeing this trickiness, venture to seek some gain from

it. And this is what Portia does too in the court at Venice –
only *she* seeks to save a man, not to save (more) money. At
a crucial time she sees, and exploits, her opportunity to
make life play her way. (Lesser characters, when matters
grow critical at other times, simply accept Fortune passively.
Nerissa, for instance, cheerfully relies on the caskets test to
bring her the 'right' husband; and Solanio and Salerio
bemoan Antonio's losses but can do nothing to alleviate
them.)

WORDS' AND DEEDS' CONTRIVING

Truth in this play is dressed up (or tricked out) in many
styles of language. For most of the time we watch the
characters using words not simply to say, but also to adorn
and decorate, what they mean. We listen to carefully *contrived* speech. We watch people who watch what they are
saying. The trait is there to some degree in all the characters,
including the minor ones like Morocco and Arragon,
Solanio and Salerio, Launcelot and the Duke. Sometimes
what is said is contrived very beautifully, expressing refined
feelings and a delicate atmosphere – as when Bassanio
approaches the caskets to make his choice, or when Lorenzo
duets with Jessica 'in such a night'. Sometimes the contrivance is bright with wit or filled with lively digression –
as in Gratiano's 'deal of nothing' or in Portia's chaffing
with Nerissa (first about suitors and later about trans-
vestism). Sometimes what is contrived is pompous posturing
(Morocco and Arragon) or well-bred prattle (Solanio and
Salerio). Sometimes speech contrives to cover sheer active
enmity: 'Why look you how you storm! I would be friends
with you and have your love . . .' or 'If thou tak'st more / Or
less than a just pound . . .'. Everywhere Shakespeare sets

people speaking artfully and art-fully; and such a variety of ways-with-words is fascinating to listen to. At one extreme there is language of such prayer-like power as Portia's speech on the quality of mercy; at another is Launcelot's petty wit-snapping and quibbling, which, as Lorenzo observes in III. 5, is sometimes enough to make one mistrust the spoken word altogether. (And this point is perhaps some justification for that scene. It is rather an empty one except when seen as an ironic introduction to the occasion when Shylock and Portia 'play upon the word' with such grim insistence: ' "Nearest his heart" – those are the very words . . .'; 'The words expressly are "a pound of flesh" '.)

But, of course, an audience does not only listen to what is said, it sees what happens; and in this play what does happen frequently *denies* what is said. Direct lies (Shylock to Antonio, Jessica to Shylock, Portia to Lorenzo) are in a way the least disturbing examples of this further doubleness within the play. Rather more so are those instances where sincere and heartfelt words are simply not borne out by the action – as when mercy is preached but not practised; or when the man who says 'I would lose all . . . to deliver you' and '. . . when this ring / Parts from this finger, then parts life from hence' neither attempts to lay down his life for his friend nor keeps his wife's first gift longer than a day or two. (His plea that he was 'enforced' to part with the ring for his honour's sake is self-regarding nonsense.) Again, the woman who describes herself as '. . . an unlessoned girl, unschooled, unpractised' turns out to be highly sophisticated, well-versed in the ways of the world, and anything but 'directed / As from her lord, her governor, her king'. Again, the character described as 'the kindest man, / The best-conditioned and unwearied spirit / In doing courtesies' derides and humiliates his business rival in public, hates him for being a Jew, and comes within spitting distance of taking his life when he has him at his mercy. 'O . . . what these Christians are' indeed! The play-in-performance shows up its 'winners' as being – in the critic Hazlitt's memorable phrase – 'hypocrites in their virtues'.

THE JEW, AND USURY

Shylock, on the other hand, is 'honest in his vices', and this is most apparent in his straight relationship with the audience. His asides come at us with disarming frankness ('I hate him for he is a Christian . . .', 'These be the Christian husbands . . .') and so does his famous comment on intolerance ('Hath not a Jew eyes . . .'). He seems to sweep us straight into his confidence. Of all the other characters, only Launcelot Gobbo speaks directly to the audience from the stage like that (a point which, when taken with Shylock's behaviour in II. 5, suggests that some aspects of the Jew's character may have been derived in Shakespeare's creative imagination from the traditionally *comic* figures of Fool and stage-miser); but Shylock gets through to us with distinctive force. He speaks his feelings plainly, in language a good deal less dressed-up than anybody else's. His malice and cruelty are blatant and the bargain-bond that he offers Antonio is a transparently vicious device. All this malevolence, like his sarcastic humour, his meanness and his hurt pride, is all too human, and only in his lust to *kill* the thing he hates does it become monstrous. He is quite open about that lust too. Through this brand of 'honesty' the impression he makes on us is the most 'personal' one in the play. And it neither hides nor excuses his villainy.

The villainy of Jews was a familiar enough idea to Shake-

speare's audience, although at the time the play was written –
between mid-1596 and mid-1598 – there were very few
Jews in England. They had been officially expelled from the
country in 1190 by Edward I. But by Shakespeare's day a
few hundred Jews of Spanish and Portuguese descent lived
in London, professing a nominal Christianity to get round
the residence laws. They lived and worked peacefully and
were generally accepted as members of the community.
Foreigners, on the other hand, who settled in London in
increasing numbers during Queen Elizabeth's reign, were
much less readily accepted. Anti-immigrant hysteria, of a
kind not unknown in England today, periodically turned to
violence. There were anti-alien riots in London in 1588,
1593 and 1595. But specifically anti-semitic feeling flared
up only once. This was in 1594 when Dr Roderigo Lopez
was tried and executed. He was a medical man, a Portuguese
Jew who had lived in England for twenty-five years with
such success in his profession that he was appointed to be
the Queen's physician. A number of the charges against
him, including that of attempting to poison Her Majesty,
may have been trumped up for political purposes; but he
was convicted of treason nonetheless, and his trial undoubtedly stirred up prejudice against Jews in general as
dark and devilish plotters of harm towards Christians. In
the popular mind this prejudice was supported less by
facts than by inherited fears and traditional attitudes, by a
background of legends, ballads and stories, and to some
extent by plays that presented Jews in this light.

As early as 1579 a lost play called *The Jew*, by an unknown author, is mentioned (by Stephen Gosson in *The
School of Abuse*) as having been presented in London.
However, Christopher Marlowe's *The Jew of Malta*, written
about 1590, was the play that had the greatest success with

the public. It was still being frequently performed by the acting companies years after its first appearance – fifteen times in ten months during 1594, the year of the Lopez affair, and eight times in six months in 1596, which made it what we would call today 'a box-office hit'. It is just possible that its very success may have incited Shakespeare to write a 'Jew' play of his own, in competition. There are some similarities between the Jews of Malta and Venice. Like Shylock, Marlowe's Barabas is rich and has an only daughter; he hates all Christians, fiercely; he plots against them; he declares himself in his true colours straight to the audience; and his lines sometimes ring to the same tune: 'We Jews can fawn like spaniels when we please; / And when we grin we bite . . .'. But the main difference between the two is more significant. Barabas is drawn in larger-than-life terms. He is a sort of impresario of wickedness, with a taste for the highly sensational. He is a savage, spectacular villain whose sheer relish for his rôle carries him near to farce. He is a cartoon figure beside the human portrait of Shylock.

Shakespeare's villain-Jew is called a bogey-man often enough by people in the play, but every time he appears we see that he is indeed a fellow man, a suffering one as well as a scheming one; and what particularly 'humanises' him is a quality that we usually find in the very young. Shakespeare 'looks both ways' at him and sees a child's direct sensibility (which is a kind of innocence) as well as the man's evil disposition (which is the fruit of his experience). Again it must be stressed that the child-like element in Shylock does not make him any the less wicked; it simply co-exists with the evil in him, as can be seen from the example of his miserliness. Like a child Shylock is passionately attached to his precious things – his house, his jewels, his ducats – as

passionately as if they were living things; like a child he
wails outright for the loss of them; like a child he swings to
and fro between intense woe over them and intense delight
over something else (any parent will surely find something
familiar in the scene with Tubal). When Shylock is hurt, he
howls; when he sees a chance to hurt back, he jumps at it;
when he can revel in doing so with impunity, he jeers at his
enemy. He is both 'little boy' and villain-Jew.

To the Elizabethans he was, no doubt, as much of a
villain for being a usurer as for being a Jew. The practice of
usury – lending money at a very high rate of interest –
was spreading widely in Shakespeare's England, as society
'developed' along increasingly urbanised and capitalist
lines. London was becoming what Venice was renowned the
world over for having once been, a great centre of international trade and commercial prosperity; and city business-
men, then as now, often needed large amounts of cash at
short notice to expand their enterprises. The usurers – who
were generally not Jews, in fact – thus became 'necessary'
to the city. Their services were also required by many
leading noblemen who were struggling to keep up appearances. The fortunes of many aristocratic families were
sinking steadily, for the traditional, country-based, feudal
economy that had sustained them was declining while a new,
competitive, town-based, capitalist system grew. Many of
the greatest courtiers of the realm were deeply, and more or
less permanently, in debt. Queen Elizabeth herself – like
Her Majesty's government today – was forced to borrow
huge sums from foreigners. (And when Shakespeare's
company of players borrowed money to build the Globe
theatre in 1599 they were burdened for years after with
heavy payments of interest on it.)

Today the idea of usury, under such polite names as

'mortgage' and 'hire purchase', causes us little dismay, so essential to our way of life do we consider it to be. But to the first Elizabethans the practice of breeding money under controlled conditions was still offensive, as an unnatural act, however expedient it might be. The Church condemned usury as sinful; the law attempted. to restrain it to an interest rate of ten per cent; but by turning a blind eye and by allowing plentiful loopholes, both Church and State permitted it to flourish. Usury was generally considered to be a grave social evil, yet society could not, it seemed, do without it. There was much popular loathing for usurers and their 'needful' services. The argument on the subject in I. 2 was undoubtedly a live issue when the play was first presented.

THE MERCHANT-VENTURER

On the other hand, the practice of venturing – that is, putting money into hazardous expeditions of trade or exploration and risking the loss of it all for the chance of a very high profit – was considered fair, even honourable, a 'natural' practice. Today, merchant-venturers are called financiers and their operations are infinitely more complex, but even in the first Elizabethan age some of them did indeed at times receive such returns as 'thrice three times the value' of the money they had put into gilt-edged ventures like Drake's expeditions. The moral distinction between this way of multiplying money by gambling with it and the usurer's method of making it increase is perhaps less evident to us now than it was to the sixteenth-century audience.

In the play, however, it is often impressed upon us that Antonio is an honourable man. At the top of his profession, he is a 'royal' merchant who tries to help his less fortunate fellow men in a humble and straightforward way. He lends money interest-free to people in need, especially those who need to get out of Shylock's clutches (III. 3. 22–4). We are told that 'a kinder gentleman treads not the earth'. He is rich, honest, generous and loyal to his friends, and an active campaigner against the Jew-usurer – in fact, a model of Elizabethan respectability. As such, and since he says and does so little in the play after Act One, he might well strike us as a worthy but rather dull soul, if Shakespeare had not also made him a sad person and, to a certain extent, the victim of his own decency (which Shylock calls his 'simplicity').

About his sadness there is no great mystery. He is by inclination solitary, by temperament sober. He seems older than most of his friends, whose self-centred enthusiasms and extravagant, pleasure-seeking ways (prodigal indeed, to judge by Bassanio's reported life-style) he does not share. He is not a marrying man, but the person he loves most in the world *is*: there's the rub. It is, of course, because he loves Bassanio so dearly (quite as dearly as Portia does) that Antonio commits himself so readily 'even to the uttermost' to helping him (just as Portia commits herself later). But when he makes this 'venture' on Bassanio's behalf, Antonio's heart, not his head, conducts the affair, making him careless of the risk he takes. When he agrees to Shylock's bond, it is as though his feelings have switched off his judgement. That is the way love takes some people – but for all its kind motive, Antonio's action is very simple-minded. It makes a marked contrast to Portia's way of dealing with Shylock; for the venture that brings her to Venice, while it is no less deeply founded on feeling, actually toughens her powers of judgement.

JUDGEMENT AND MERCY

'Seven times tried that judgement is / That did never choose amiss' says the scroll in the silver casket. But where in the world may judgement as pure, as refined, as that be found? Certainly not in Belmont or Venice. In most obvious ways the suitors Morocco and Arragon 'choose amiss'. Antonio's 'choice' in accepting a bond with an obvious death-wish built into it is scarcely any better-judged. Bassanio at least has the wit to choose the right casket, but not to stick to the right course when he is asked to part with his wife's ring. And Shylock's bloodthirsty insistence on having his pound of flesh, against all persuasions, is altogether 'amiss'. If all judgement were as frail as this, the world would soon be in a hopeless state. Fortunately, the play suggests that some finer power can exist in human nature, and this it embodies in Portia. She judges matters, as she judges character, with insight and a deft touch. She is more acutely poised than any of the men in the play. Her temperament, like that of all Shakespeare's heroines, is typically feminine, while her character includes many of the play's main masculine qualities. She can be as determined, as devious and as outspoken as Shylock, as dignified as Antonio, as lyrical-romantic as Bassanio, and she has something of Gratiano's yen for earthy humour, with a considerable relish for playing upon a tricksy word. Her nature seems to be equal to every occasion. When she speaks in court of the quality of mercy, she is the expression of possible, positive grace in humankind; while the judgement she embodies is strong enough to counteract the destructive menace embodied in Shylock, for she is of an undaunted mettle.

Portia is a living assurance that something like true judgement can operate effectively, when helped by Love and Good Fortune, to save humanity from its own frailty (and worse). 'Something *like* true judgement', not the thing itself – that is the point. Portia's judgement is a good deal, but it is also a good deal less than perfect; and our discomfort in the outcome of the trial is, among other things, the acknowledgement of this. An ideal judgement would not merely force the law on men, it would do justice to their human condition; and this is not what happens when a weight of misfortune and inhumanity is lifted from the shoulders of one man and transferred to another. True justice lies beyond the exigencies of life-saving and the equation of 'an eye for an eye and a tooth for a tooth'. It could appear in Venice only if the positive grace in life, the quality of mercy that Portia describes so eloquently, were to operate as a real force within the play. It does not do so. Mercy remains at the level of spiritual injunction, a noble possibility which we meet in moving words: 'We do pray for mercy, / And that same prayer doth teach us all / To render the deeds of mercy'; but the words do not come alive in action in the play; mercy is not rendered real, not realised, in deed.

When, in later plays, Shakespeare did make the quality of mercy real in deeply convincing human action – in, for instance, *Measure for Measure*, in *King Lear*, in *The Winter's Tale* – his vision of evil and of human frailty had grown too penetrating, too scathing, to be contained any longer within the conventional resources of comedy. For *The Merchant of Venice* he stuck to those resources, and so the play behaves correctly as comic drama – human follies are exposed in it, nobody dies in it, there is a considerable display of wit and caricature, and the ups-and-downs of several love-affairs prove entertaining. But the greatness of the play lies in something else: in its particular degree of candour. Its version of 'the way things are' does not sacrifice truth for the sake of a smoother style (as it might have done, for instance, by making its Christian gentlemen into thoroughly 'nice' people). It does not settle down as a light diversion from the real world, an escapist entertainment; but rather it grows more and more realistic in the way it treats human nature, as it goes on. It will not resolve matters into a respectable harmony at the close, but leaves us in the garden at Belmont with the form of a happy ending echoing with reminders of the *un*happiness we have seen in Venice. (The trial and its issue are recalled more and more strongly in the dialogue of Act Five as it draws to its close.) So we can hardly leave the play feeling that all's well that ends well. Shakespeare's perspective is truer to life than that. He presents the world candidly as a tricky place that can be highly attractive and potentially lethal at one and the same time; a place where our human frailty is both comical and appalling; a hazardous place, not too easy to live well in, since the bonds that seem to be our life-lines can change so suddenly into traps.

CONJECTURES AND SOURCES

If one of Shakespeare's motives in writing this play was indeed to compete with Marlowe's highly successful *The Jew of Malta*, then he may have been working in more of a hurry than was his wont; and, to save time, he may in places have borrowed or re-worked material from some of his earlier plays. Much of the talk between Portia and Nerissa in I. 2, for instance, seems modelled on a discussion of suitors in I. 2 of *The Two Gentlemen of Verona*; and the character of Launcelot Gobbo closely resembles that of

Launce in the same play. Equally, the character of Gratiano, with his exuberance, his mocking wit and his often bawdy gusto, may have come largely ready-made from left-over material for Mercutio in *Romeo and Juliet*; and the love-talk of Bassanio and Portia, and of Lorenzo and Jessica, is on occasions very close in style and tone to some of the poetry of those famous earlier lovers. Such resemblances – when considered along with a number of minor inconsistencies in the text and those brief scenes that seem to have been cobbled up rather than integrated (the two Gobbos in II. 2; all of III. 5) – such things make a theory that Shakespeare was hurrying to furnish his players with their script seem quite attractive; but they are nothing like proof of it.

More likely to be true is the conjecture that Shakespeare based the main elements of his play on a tale from a collection by Ser Giovanni, published in Italy in 1558 and called *Il Pecorone* (which means literally 'The Great Ram' and figuratively 'The Simpleton'). The tale had been written a long time before it was printed, and by the time Shakespeare wrote *The Merchant* it was nearly two hundred years old. *Il Pecorone* included the wooing at Belmont, the flesh-bond with the Jew in Venice, the trial triumphantly conducted by the lady-in-disguise, and the ring-trick; and Shakespeare's play corresponds closely with it in a great number of details. Shakespeare probably read the tale in Italian, for no Elizabethan translation of it is known. A modern one can be found as an appendix in the Arden Shakespeare edition of the play, and it is well worth reading. It is a spirited yarn, of a kind that many a real-life Gratiano would no doubt have enjoyed.

In the tale, Giannetto is the centre of attention for most of the time, as his opposite number in the play, Bassanio, is not: and this is one of a number of noteworthy differences between the two works. The most striking ones occur in the character of Portia. In Ser Giovanni's version 'the lady of Belmonte' is an anonymous *widow*, and a very merry one – a kind of worldly temptress. The suitors who sail into her port have to prove themselves to be 'the right man' for her in a quite different way from those who come to Portia (the caskets do not feature in the Italian story at all) and when, by her contrivance, they fail her wooing-test, she seizes their ships and all the contents. (Thus in the story the suitors run the risk of shipwreck in person, while Bassanio in the play runs it at secondhand.) The lady of Belmonte is quite as rich and just as resourceful as Portia, but her character lacks altogether the spiritual dimension of Shakespeare's heroine. Similarly the story gives Giannetto a more down-to-earth, substantial quality than Bassanio has in the play. Both authors present the young man as an impoverished, well-bred, fortune-seeking prodigal, but Giannetto's accomplishments in the courtly and manly arts are given much the fuller treatment (and his strong point is perseverance, since he only wins the lady at the third attempt).

Two other differences between the play and its probable main source may be mentioned here. First, in the Italian tale the merchant of Venice is paternal in his relationship with Giannetto; he is his godfather, and he takes the orphaned young man to be his own son. In the play the relationship is different; Antonio is simply the 'lover' of Bassanio, to whom he is bound in 'god-like amity'. Secondly, Ser Giovanni does not let his Christian merchant crush the Jew with punishing conditions at the end of the court scene. In his version the defeated Jew tears up his bond in a fury and storms out, flesh- and ducat-less but unbowed.

Shakespeare habitually drew material for a play from a

number of sources – the trial-by-caskets that he put in place of Ser Giovanni's wooing-test, for instance, probably came from another collection of tales, medieval Latin ones, called the *Gesta Romanorum* and published in English in the late sixteenth century – but the psychology of amity and enmity that he explores in the particular personalities of Portia and Shylock is all his own inspiration. They compel our attention and imagination in quite distinct ways. Portia commands our ear, in a wide assortment of tones and manners. She is, as it were, a fine spirit rendered vocal, and we listen to her with respect – and sometimes with amusement and, occasionally, with dismay. But we take Shylock on our pulses. He involves us not just in listening but in being. We feel his experience with a direct pressure, and the expression of it seems at times to be nearer to the mode of Shakespeare's 'problem plays' and tragedies than to comedy. It is not altogether surprising that in the theatre the play seems to belong chiefly to Shylock, for he 'lives' in it more affectingly than any other character. It is as though the passion of enmity has stirred the dramatist's creative imagination into sharper life than the passion of amity. Or, to put it another way, Shakespeare acts on us through Shylock and recites to us through Portia.

THEN AND NOW

The Merchant of Venice seems to have pleased audiences in Shakespeare's day, and it has remained popular in ours – though productions have sometimes obscured the candid ambivalence in its treatment of its main themes (a treatment that Shakespeare intensified when he looked further into Honour's relations with Prodigality in *Henry IV*, *Part* 1 and *Henry IV*, *Part* 2, which he probably wrote just after *The*

Merchant). Although 'the most excellent Historie of the *Merchant of Venice*' was 'divers times acted' before 1600, only one production remains on record in the whole of the seventeenth century. On 10 February 1605 Shakespeare's company performed the play before their patron King James at court, and pleased His Majesty so well with it as to be commanded to repeat it forty-eight hours later. Since then the play has pleased the public in a wide variety of interpretations, but for the first forty years of the eighteenth century it was not performed professionally at all. During that time a highly popular and thoroughly rewritten version called *The Jew of Venice* (which, as it happens, is an alternative title given to the play in its first entry in the Stationers' Register in 1598) held the stage. This version by George Granville must have flattered theatregoers' idea of dramatic Good Form, but in giving the public what it wanted it so 'tidied up' Shakespeare's play as to make it into a different work altogether. Several scenes were cut out, large tracts of verse were omitted or restyled, much of the characterisation was transformed (Bassanio's somewhat hollow rôle, for instance, was filled out and ennobled, and Shylock's was made a vehicle for a famous farcical comedian of the day), a full-blown masque was introduced, and the play's disquieting tensions were muted into mere simple contrasts. Something nearer to Shakespeare returned in 1741 when Charles Macklin restored most of the original text and, though himself a comedian, played Shylock 'straight' with great success at Drury Lane – since when *The Merchant of Venice* has had a regular and popular place in the repertoires of professional theatre. In 1814 Edmund Kean's triumph in the part of Shylock marked the start of his notable career as a tragic actor, and throughout the nineteenth century the rôle was a star part for a succession of actors and actor-managers, who often eclipsed the rest of the play with their grand manner in it. Such out-and-out tragic style must have unbalanced the play very severely.

In modern performances the stress-patterns of the play as a whole, rather than those of the Jew alone, have tended to emerge more clearly – though the caustic and ambivalent flavour that emerges with them has not always been considered a virtue by critics. A reviewer in *The Times*, for instance, while praising an actor for making Shylock 'a man of middle stature – neither a giant . . . nor a cur . . .' found the play itself to be a 'strangely arbitrary' work that was like a badly cut garment, 'ill-fitting . . . with brilliant embroideries'.

Candour, not arbitrariness, makes the play disquieting (rather than ill-fitting). If we take it as it is, and not as the play we might prefer it to be, it will not comfort us about human nature. It exposes instead the 'double' quality in that nature, which renders us all so vulnerable. By judicious mistrust of false appearance the hand of a Portia may be won; but only by simple trust in the false appearance of Portia may the life of an Antonio be saved. In the end everything in the garden is not lovely but tricky. In such a world it is easier to do wrong than to do right, and, in doing either, degrees of pain cannot be avoided. That is what the play real-ises. It says what a modern writer of serious comedy, James Saunders, declares, equally disarmingly, in the words of a character in his play *Next Time I'll Sing To You*:

There lies behind everything, and you can believe this or not as you wish, a certain quality which we may call grief. It's always there, just under the surface, just behind the façade, sometimes very nearly exposed, so that you can see dimly the shape of it. . . .

A NOTE ON THE TEXT AND THE DATE OF THE PLAY . . .

The Merchant of Venice was published for the first time in a Quarto edition of 1600. The text was quite carefully printed, and it seems possible that the printers worked from Shakespeare's own papers (or a source very close to them) rather than from a playhouse copy of the script. When the play was printed in the First Folio edition of the collected works in 1623 the text was set from a lightly corrected version of the first Quarto that may have been used in the playhouse. However, the Folio text introduced some new misprints, as well as correcting earlier ones. So the present edition is based chiefly on the first Quarto, with additions and emendations chiefly from the First Folio.

The play must have been complete by 22 July 1598, when it first appeared in the Stationers' Register (which was the Elizabethan way of declaring a copyright). If, as seems very likely, Salerio's reference to 'my wealthy *Andrew*' (I. 1. 27) alludes to the large Spanish ship *St Andrew* captured by the English while she was aground in Cadiz harbour in July 1596, then August of that year would be the earliest date at which the play could have been written.

. . . AND A FINAL NOTE ON SOME OF THE NOTES

Shakespeare wrote the play for his company to perform in what had been 'the first permanent professional public playhouse of the modern world', known first as the Theatre, in Shoreditch, and later (when it had been dismantled and re-built in 1598–9) as the Globe, on Bankside. It seems reasonable to believe that the projecting stage of this playhouse was roofed, that the back of it had a door at each side with a curtained enclosure (the inner stage) between them, and that above this there was a balcony, or gallery, with windows over the doors. The present editor hopes that some of his notes will help the reader to see in his own mind's eye a performance in this theatre.

THE MERCHANT OF VENICE

THE CHARACTERS

ANTONIO, a merchant of Venice

BASSANIO, his friend, and suitor to Portia

GRATIANO
SALERIO } their friends
SOLANIO

LORENZO, another friend of Antonio and Bassanio, in love with Jessica

LEONARDO, servant to Bassanio

LAUNCELOT GOBBO, a clown, servant first to Shylock and then to Bassanio

OLD GOBBO, father of Launcelot

SHYLOCK, a Jew and a moneylender

JESSICA, his daughter

TUBAL, another Jew, friend of Shylock

PORTIA, an heiress of Belmont, later disguised as a lawyer

NERISSA, her waiting-woman, later disguised as her clerk

PRINCE OF MOROCCO
PRINCE OF ARRAGON } suitors to Portia

BALTHASAR
STEPHANO } servants to Portia

DUKE OF VENICE

Magnificoes of Venice, Officers of the Court of Justice, a Gaoler, Servants, Musicians and Attendants

ACT ONE, scene 1

Venice *To Shakespeare's audience the city was famous and fascinating as a rich international trading centre and a trend-setter in culture, fashion and luxury. Its glory had declined by the 1590s, but the reputation lingered on, and London, as an expanding centre of commerce, aspired to it.*

Salerio and Solanio *Similar-sounding names for similar characters. Two friends – or hangers-on.– of the merchant of Venice, they are never lost for words. Some early editions give some of their lines in later scenes to a third friend, named Salarino.*

[1] in sooth *truly*

[2, 3, 4] it *his sadness – a heavy state of depression*

[5] I am to learn *I have no idea*

[6] a want-wit *a lack-brain; a fool*

[7] I . . . myself *or, as we might say, 'I can hardly tell what to make of myself'.*

[9] argosies *large merchant ships*

  portly sail *sails both swelling and stately*

[10] signiors and rich burghers *gentlemen and respectable, wealthy citizens. Salerio's comparison, aimed perhaps at flattering Antonio, suggests the superior air of these people.*

[11] pageants *wagons, elaborately decorated with large set-pieces for festive processions (as in carnivals these days)*

[12–14] petty traffickers . . . woven wings *the small trading boats that bob and dip (as if bowing respectfully) in the wash made by the argosies when these speed by under full sail*

[15] venture *a risky capitalist enterprise in foreign trade*

[16] affections *thoughts and concern*

[17] still *always*

[19] roads *anchorages*

[21] ventures *see [15]*

[23] blow me to an ague *send me into a fit of the shivers*

[26] flats *sandbanks*

[27] *Andrew a well-known name for a big ship in Shakespeare's day: but see also Introduction, p. 24.*

[28–9] Vailing . . . burial *Salerio imagines the wrecked ship beaten right over on her side, the tip of her mast touching the sand that will eventually engulf her.*

ACT ONE

Scene 1. *Enter* ANTONIO, SALERIO *and* SOLANIO

ANTONIO In sooth I know not why I am so sad.
It wearies me; you say it wearies you –
But how I caught it, found it, or came by it,
What stuff 'tis made of, whereof it is born,
I am to learn;
And such a want-wit sadness makes of me
That I have much ado to know myself.

SALERIO Your mind is tossing on the ocean,
There where your argosies with portly sail
(Like signiors and rich burghers on the flood,   10
Or as it were the pageants of the sea)
Do overpeer the petty traffickers
That curtsy to them, do them reverence,
As they fly by them with their woven wings.

SOLANIO Believe me, sir, had I such venture forth,
The better part of my affections would
Be with my hopes abroad. I should be still
Plucking the grass to know where sits the wind,
Peering in maps for ports and piers and roads;
And every object that might make me fear   20
Misfortune to my ventures, out of doubt
Would make me sad.

SALERIO   My wind cooling my broth
Would blow me to an ague when I thought
What harm a wind too great might do at sea.
I should not see the sandy hour-glass run
But I should think of shallows and of flats,
And see my wealthy *Andrew* docked in sand,
Vailing her high top lower than her ribs

THE MERCHANT OF VENICE

[30] edifice *building*

[32] gentle vessel *both 'noble ship' and 'delicate container'*

[35–6] And . . . nothing *He breaks off his flowing description to show with a single sharp gesture how in one moment ('word') the great value of ship and cargo ('this') may be ruined.*

[36–8] Shall . . . sad *'Since I can imagine the possibility of such a wreck I can surely grasp the fact that if such a thing were actually to happen it would make me sad.' Though exaggerated in manner, Salerio's remarks evoke real risks that Antonio runs; such disasters do beset him later.*

[41–5] *Compare these lines with ll. 177–80. Antonio is polite on the subject with Solanio and Salerio – and frank later with Bassanio.*

[41] fortune *both 'wealth' and 'fate' together (see Introduction, p. 6)*

[42] ventures *see* [15]

bottom *ship*

[43] my whole estate *all that I own and am*

[44] upon *dependent upon*

fortune *see* [41]

[50] two-headed Janus *the Roman god of exits and entrances, with one merry face and one sad one*

[52] evermore peep through their eyes *always screw up their eyes in mirth. (Perhaps Solanio has seen Gratiano coming.)*

[54] vinegar aspect *sour looks. Baffled in his efforts to diagnose Antonio's melancholy, and to cheer him up, Solanio half-seriously rebukes him.*

To kiss her burial. Should I go to church
And see the holy edifice of stone   30
And not bethink me straight of dangerous rocks,
Which touching but my gentle vessel's side
Would scatter all her spices on the stream,
Enrobe the roaring waters with my silks –
And in a word, but even now worth this,
And now worth nothing? Shall I have the
   thought
To think on this, and shall I lack the thought
That such a thing bechanced would make me
   sad?
But tell not me – I know Antonio
Is sad to think upon his merchandise.   40

ANTONIO Believe me, no. I thank my fortune for it,
My ventures are not in one bottom trusted,
Nor to one place; nor is my whole estate
Upon the fortune of this present year.
Therefore my merchandise makes me not sad.

SOLANIO Why then you are in love.

ANTONIO   Fie, fie!

SOLANIO Not in love neither? Then let us say you
   are sad
Because you are not merry; and 'twere as easy
For you to laugh and leap, and say you are
   merry
Because you are not sad. Now by two-headed
   Janus,   50
Nature hath framed strange fellows in her time;
Some that will evermore peep through their
   eyes
And laugh like parrots at a bagpiper,
And other of such vinegar aspect

[56] Nestor *the oldest, most grave and venerable of the Greek leaders at Troy. (When such as he found a thing funny, it must have been so!)*

[57] kinsman *Usually a kinsman is a male relation, but such a connection between Bassanio and Antonio is not indicated anywhere else in the play; the sense of 'companion' is probably meant.*

[59, 61] better company/worthier friends *Antonio probably looks more cheerful at Bassanio's approach, and Solanio and Salerio may be a little piqued at 'favouritism'.*

[61] prevented *forestalled*

[62] Your . . . regard *A courtesy-remark: 'I value your friendship very highly'.*

[64] embrace th'occasion *seize the opportunity*

[66] laugh *meet to enjoy ourselves. Entertainment is a major feature of life for Bassanio and his cronies – their evening's amusement, for instance, is already planned (see l. 71).*

[67] You . . . so? *In modern idiom this remark amounts to 'We hardly see anything of you these days. Can't we change that?'.*

[70] We two will leave you *A strong, but fruitless, hint to Gratiano.*

[74] respect upon *concern for*

[75] They . . . care *Gratiano may have in mind the familiar biblical saying 'For whosoever will save his life shall lose it' (Matthew 16: 25).*

[76] marvellously changed *A typically over-effusive remark of Gratiano's, elaborating on 'You look not well'. He cheerily suggests that Antonio looks extraordinarily miserable!*

[77] hold *regard*

That they'll not show their teeth in way of
    smile
Though Nestor swear the jest be laughable.

Enter BASSANIO, LORENZO *and* GRATIANO

Here comes Bassanio your most noble kinsman,
Gratiano, and Lorenzo. Fare ye well;
We leave you now with better company.

SALERIO I would have stayed till I had made you
    merry,   60
If worthier friends had not prevented me.

ANTONIO Your worth is very dear in my regard.
I take it your own business calls on you,
And you embrace th'occasion to depart.

SALERIO [*To* BASSANIO, LORENZO *and* GRATIANO]
    Good morrow, my good lords.

BASSANIO Good signiors both, when shall we laugh?
    Say, when?
You grow exceeding strange – must it be
    so?

SALERIO We'll make our leisures to attend on yours.
                  [*Exeunt* SALERIO *and* SOLANIO

LORENZO My Lord Bassanio, since you have found
    Antonio,
We two will leave you; but at dinner-time   70
I pray you have in mind where we must meet.

BASSANIO I will not fail you.

GRATIANO You look not well, Signior Antonio.
You have too much respect upon the world:
They lose it that do buy it with much care.
Believe me, you are marvellously changed.

ANTONIO I hold the world but as the world,
    Gratiano –

[78–9] A stage . . . one *This was a commonly-held view of the world in Shakespeare's day. He expanded it in a famous speech – 'All the world's a stage – in* As You Like It *II. 6. 139–66.*

[79] play the fool *The name 'Gratiano' belonged to a fool – the comic doctor in the popular Italian* commedia dell'arte *(a kind of sixteenth-century improvised pantomime). In the following 'exhortation' against melancholy silence Gratiano addresses Antonio in mock-medical style, and so 'plays the fool'. literally (rather than in our modern sense of the term).*

[81, 82] liver/heart *It was supposed that these organs governed love and passion in the human constitution. Groans and sighs deadened life, it was thought, by draining blood from the heart.*

[84] Sit . . . alabaster *remain as cold and still as the effigy carved on his grandfather's tomb*

[85] sleep when he wakes *seem asleep (by being silent and impassive) when in fact he is awake*

jaundice *a disease which yellows the skin (once thought to arise from a perturbed state of mind)*

[87] (I . . . speaks) *A mollifying comment, for Gratiano realises that he is being very cheeky (in going on to imply that Antonio's melancholy is mere affectation).*

[89] cream and mantle *acquire a thick skin (by never being moved)*

[90–4] wilful . . . bark *deliberately cultivate an over-solemn manner in order to acquire a reputation for being wise, serious and deeply insightful – as if they were saying (to the world) 'I am as wise and important as the Greek oracle (whose inspiration came from the gods) and when I do speak I should be listened to with the utmost respect'*

[98] dam *Probably a pun with 'damn'. The sense would then be that if ever these pseudo-wise men did speak they would (i) stuff their hearers' ears almost full with nonsense and (ii) thereby incite the listeners to call them fools – a response which would invite damnation according to the New Testament (Matthew 5: 22)*

[100] I'll . . . time *It is possible that Gratiano breaks off his sermon because Antonio is hardly paying any attention by this time.*

[101–2] But . . . opinion *Don't seek to impress people by keeping sadly silent, for that sort of reputation is worth no more than a small and silly fish.*

A stage, where every man must play a part,
And mine a sad one.

GRATIANO   Let me play the fool!
With mirth and laughter let old wrinkles come,   80
And let my liver rather heat with wine
Than my heart cool with mortifying groans.
Why should a man whose blood is warm
    within
Sit like his grandsire cut in alabaster,
Sleep when he wakes, and creep into the
    jaundice
By being peevish? I tell thee what, Antonio
(I love thee, and 'tis my love that speaks)
There are a sort of men whose visages
Do cream and mantle like a standing pond,
And do a wilful stillness entertain   90
With purpose to be dressed in an opinion
Of wisdom, gravity, profound conceit –
As who should say, 'I am Sir Oracle,
And when I ope my lips, let no dog bark!'
O my Antonio, I do know of these
That therefore only are reputed wise
For saying nothing; when I am very sure
If they should speak, would almost dam those
    ears
Which, hearing them, would call their brothers
    fools.
I'll tell thee more of this another time.   100
But fish not with this melancholy bait
For this fool gudgeon, this opinion.
Come, good Lorenzo. [*To* ANTONIO] Fare ye
    well awhile;
I'll end my exhortation after dinner.

[110] grow *become*
      for this gear *in return for the load of stuff (and nonsense)*
you have just told me

[112] neat's tongue *ox tongue (a moist meat in the raw)*
      not vendible *unsaleable (i.e. whom no one will marry).*
This parting couplet is the first of Gratiano's several dirty jokes in
the play. Antonio misses the point.
[115] reasons *intelligent points*
[117] chaff *'Chaffing' his friends is a favourite occupation of*
Gratiano, only half-approved of by Bassanio (see II. 2. 171-9).
      ere *before*
[120] the same *she*
[121] pilgrimage *The word implies that the lady has the quality*
of a saint – and the implication is repeated often in the play.
[120-122] Well ... of *Is it the knowledge that Bassanio is*
bound ('... you swore ...') to leave him that has made Antonio so
sad?
[123] *In the speech beginning here and in his next one, Bassanio*
'covers up' his faults with a very roundabout, diplomatic way of
talking.
[124-6] How ... continuance *what harm I have done myself*
by living more extravagantly than I could afford to
[125] a more swelling port *Compare [9] and [10]*
[127-8] abridged ... rate *forced to cut down my grand life-*
style
[129] to come fairly off from *to settle fully and properly*
[130] my time, something too prodigal *my rather too lavish*
youth

LORENZO [*To* ANTONIO] Well, we will leave you then
    till dinner-time.

    I must be one of these same dumb wise men,
    For Gratiano never lets me speak.

GRATIANO Well, keep me company but two years
    more,

    Thou shalt not know the sound of thine own
    tongue.

ANTONIO Fare you well. I'll grow a talker for this
    gear.   110

GRATIANO Thanks i'faith – for silence is only
    commendable

    In a neat's tongue dried and a maid not
    vendible.

                [*Exeunt* GRATIANO *and* LORENZO

ANTONIO Is that anything now?

BASSANIO Gratiano speaks an infinite deal of nothing
– more than any man in all Venice. His reasons
are as two grains of wheat hid in two bushels of
chaff: you shall seek all day ere you find them,
and when you have them they are not worth the
search.

ANTONIO Well, tell me now, what lady is the same 120
    To whom you swore a secret pilgrimage
    That you today promised to tell me of?

BASSANIO 'Tis not unknown to you, Antonio,
    How much I have disabled mine estate
    By something showing a more swelling port
    Than my faint means would grant continuance.
    Nor do I now make moan to be abridged
    From such a noble rate; but my chief care
    Is to come fairly off from the great debts
    Wherein my time, something too prodigal,   130

[131] gaged *bound*

[133] a warranty *permission*
[134] To unburden *to unload (by explaining)*

[137] still *always*

[140] occasions *needs*

[141] shaft *arrow*

[142] his fellow of the self-same flight *an identical arrow*
[143] advisèd *careful*

[145-6] I . . . innocence *In this claim to 'pure innocence'
(complete sincerity) Bassanio blandly tries to disguise the fact that he
has come with the firm intention of asking Antonio for a further loan.*
[147] wilful *impulsive; headstrong*

[149] self *same*

[151, 152] or . . . Or *either . . . or*
[152] your latter hazard *your latest loan (which involves you
in further risk)*
[154-5] and . . . circumstance *you merely waste time by treating
me as a person who needs to be wooed through such devious approaches.
(Understandably, Antonio is impatient with Bassanio's 'tact' – and
tactics!)*
[157] In . . . uttermost *in doubting that I would be willing to do
the utmost in my power for you*

Hath left me gaged. To you, Antonio,
I owe the most in money and in love;
And from your love I have a warranty
To unburden all my plots and purposes
How to get clear of all the debts I owe.

ANTONIO I pray you, good Bassanio, let me know it;
And if it stand as you yourself still do,
Within the eye of honour, be assured
My purse, my person, my extremest means
Lie all unlocked to your occasions.   140

BASSANIO In my schooldays, when I had lost one shaft,
I shot his fellow of the self-same flight
The self-same way, with more advisèd watch,
To find the other forth; and by adventuring both,
I oft found both. I urge this childhood proof
Because what follows is pure innocence.
I owe you much, and (like a wilful youth)
That which I owe is lost: but if you please
To shoot another arrow that self way
Which you did shoot the first, I do not doubt   150
(As I will watch the aim) or to find both
Or bring your latter hazard back again,
And thankfully rest debtor for the first.

ANTONIO You know me well, and herein spend but time
To wind about my love with circumstance,
And out of doubt you do me now more wrong
In making question of my uttermost
Than if you had made waste of all I have.
Then do but say to me what I should do

[161] prest unto it   *quite ready to do it*

[162] richly left   *who has inherited great wealth*

[163] fairer than that word   *better still*

[164] virtues   *talents and abilities, as well as fine moral qualities*

[166] nothing undervalued   *no less in worth*

[167] Brutus' Portia   *Marcus Brutus' spouse was famous as a model wife – clever, loyal and courageous. Shakespeare presents her thus in his play* Julius Caesar

[170] locks   *hair*

[171] golden fleece   *Alluding to the legend of Jason who brought back the golden fleece from the eastern shores of the Black Sea ('Colchos' strond') in his ship the* Argo.

[172] seat   *estate*

[174–5] means . . . them   *money enough to appear to be as well-off as her other suitors*

[176] I . . . thrift   *I have in advance such a strong notion of success. (The word 'thrift' also carries the sense of 'financial profit' which is, no doubt, strongly in Bassanio's mind.)*

[177] questionless   *certainly. (It seems that Bassanio has not yet heard of the test of the caskets, devised since he visited Belmont.)*

[179] commodity   *merchandise, goods*

[180] a present sum   *ready money*

[182] racked   *stretched (as in torture)*

[184] presently   *immediately*

[186] of my trust or for my sake   *formally on credit or as a friendly loan*

That in your knowledge may by me be done, 160
And I am prest unto it. Therefore speak.
BASSANIO In Belmont is a lady richly left,
And she is fair and, fairer than that word,
Of wondrous virtues. Sometimes from her eyes
I did receive fair speechless messages.
Her name is Portia, nothing undervalued
To Cato's daughter, Brutus' Portia;
Nor is the wide world ignorant of her worth,
For the four winds blow in from every coast
Renownèd suitors, and her sunny locks 170
Hang on her temples like a golden fleece,
Which makes her seat of Belmont Colchos'
    strond,
And many Jasons come in quest of her.
O my Antonio, had I but the means
To hold a rival place with one of them,
I have a mind presages me such thrift
That I should questionless be fortunate.
ANTONIO Thou know'st that all my fortunes are at
    sea;
Neither have I money, nor commodity,
To raise a present sum. Therefore go forth – 180
Try what my credit can in Venice do.
That shall be racked even to the uttermost
To furnish thee to Belmont to fair Portia.
Go presently inquire – and so will I –
Where money is; and I no question make
To have it of my trust or for my sake.
                              [*Exeunt*

ACT ONE, scene 2

The play moves to Belmont, into prose and (as if to endorse Bassanio's sunny description of Portia) into a brighter air – for the ladies' conversation is sprightly, down-to-earth and 'open'; and Portia's wit makes puns galore!

Nerissa   *Her name implies that she is dark-haired (in Italian 'nero' means black) to enhance, by contrast, fair Portia.*

[1] troth   *faith*

[2] aweary of this great world   *An echo of Antonio's opening sentiments in the previous scene – but set in a far lighter key. See [52].*

[3] you would be   *you really would be tired of the world (instead of just saying you are so)*

[5] for aught I see   *as far as I can see*

[6] surfeit   *grow glutted*

[7] mean   *slight, petty*

[8] to be seated in the mean   *to have neither too much nor too little in life.*

superfluity . . . longer   *those who have much more than they need age faster than those who have just enough*

[11] sentences   *maxims, wise sayings (in Latin, sententiae)*

pronounced   *spoken. Shakespeare may intend a pun with the sense of a judge 'pronouncing sentence'. Portia seems familiar with the ways of the law; she uses a number of legal terms in this scene.*

[14] chapels had been churches   *(though anyone can see how to improve the world with good works in theory) in practice it's easier to build a small chapel than a big church*

[16] divine   *preacher*

[19] The brain . . . decree   *Portia is responding to Nerissa's remarks by 'pronouncing' a string of 'sentences' in her turn (and this one could be regarded as a motto for the play as a whole!).*

[20] the blood   *one's emotional nature (as opposed to one's intellectual nature, seated in the brain)*

hot temper   *passionate disposition*

[21] hare   *The Elizabethans hunted hares with nets in wintertime.*

[23] this reasoning . . . husband   *all this wise talk cannot help me at all to find a husband. (She is 'aweary' because only too aware of how she is 'curbed by the will of a dead father'.)*

[25] I would   *I would like*

[26] will   *desire*

[27] will   *testament*

[29] ever   *unfailingly*

[29–30] holy men . . . inspirations   *It was popularly believed that men saw things particularly 'rightly' just before they died – hence Nerissa's confidence that all will be decided for the best by the 'lottery'.*

Scene 2. *Enter* PORTIA *with her waiting-woman,*
NERISSA

PORTIA By my troth, Nerissa, my little body is
aweary of this great world.

NERISSA You would be, sweet madam, if your
miseries were in the same abundance as your good
fortunes are – and yet for aught I see, they are as
sick that surfeit with too much as they that
starve with nothing. It is no mean happiness,
therefore, to be seated in the mean: superfluity
comes sooner by white hairs, but competency
lives longer.   10

PORTIA Good sentences, and well pronounced.

NERISSA They would be better if well followed.

PORTIA If to do were as easy as to know what were
good to do, chapels had been churches, and poor
men's cottages princes' palaces. It is a good
divine that follows his own instructions. I can
easier teach twenty what were good to be done,
than be one of the twenty to follow mine own
teaching. The brain may devise laws for the
blood, but a hot temper leaps o'er a cold decree;   20
such a hare is Madness (the youth) to skip o'er
the meshes of Good Counsel (the cripple) – but
this reasoning is not in the fashion to choose me a
husband. O me, the word 'choose'! I may
neither choose who I would nor refuse who I
dislike, so is the will of a living daughter curbed
by the will of a dead father. Is it not hard,
Nerissa, that I cannot choose one nor refuse none?

NERISSA Your father was ever virtuous; and holy
men at their death have good inspirations.   30

[31-2] **these three chests** *Probably a homely reference and not an indication that the caskets are actually on the stage in this scene.*

[38] **over-name them** *run through the list*

[40] **level at my affection** *(you can) guess how I like them*

[41] **Neapolitan prince** *The Neapolitans were particularly good horsemen.*

[42] **a colt** *a foolish, somewhat graceless, young man*

[43-4] **a great . . parts** *a particular point in his own favour*

[47] **County** *Count*

[48-9] **as who . . . choose!** *as if to say 'if you won't take me as your husband, then pick anyone!'*

[51] **the weeping philosopher** *Heraclitus of Ephesus, a by-word for brooding solemnity in his view of the world*

[52] **unmannerly sadness** *anti-social seriousness (with, possibly, a pun on 'unmanly')*

[63] **throstle** *thrush*

[63-4] **falls straight** *immediately starts*

Therefore the lottery that he hath devised in these three chests of gold, silver and lead – whereof who chooses his meaning chooses you – will no doubt never be chosen by any rightly but one who you shall rightly love. But what warmth is there in your affection towards any of these princely suitors that are already come?

PORTIA I pray thee over-name them, and as thou namest them I will describe them, and according to my description level at my affection. 40

NERISSA First, there is the Neapolitan prince.

PORTIA Ay, that's a colt indeed, for he doth nothing but talk of his horse, and he makes it a great appropriation to his own good parts that he can shoe him himself. I am much afeard my lady his mother played false with a smith.

NERISSA Then is there the County Palatine.

PORTIA He doth nothing but frown – as who should say, 'And you will not have me, choose!' He hears merry tales and smiles not. I fear he will 50 prove the weeping philosopher when he grows old, being so full of unmannerly sadness in his youth. I had rather be married to a death's-head with a bone in his mouth than to either of these. God defend me from these two!

NERISSA How say you by the French lord, Monsieur Le Bon?

PORTIA God made him, and therefore let him pass for a man. In truth, I know it is a sin to be a mocker, but he!—Why, he hath a horse better 60 than the Neapolitan's, a better bad habit of frowning than the Count Palatine; he is every man in no man. If a throstle sing, he falls

47

[73–4] **you will come into the court and swear** *you will bear me witness*

[75] **a proper man's picture** *that is to say, he is 'a handsome fellow, but he can't talk'*

[76] **a dumb-show** *a mime*

[77] **suited** *both 'dressed' and 'put together'*

doublet *jacket*

[78] **round hose** *baggy trousers (or breeches). (The picture of the typical Englishman abroad as an amusing hotch-potch of fashion – and a hopeless linguist – is still current!)*

[82] **a neighbourly charity** *A topical irony. England and Scotland had been on bad terms for some time when this play appeared . . .*

[85–6] **Frenchman became his surety** *. . . and France repeatedly promised to help Scotland in the quarrels. (The guarantor – 'surety' – of a legal agreement signed his name under that of the person he supported in the bond.)*

[93] **and the worst fall that ever fell** *come what may ('and' meaning 'if')*

[94] **make shift** *contrive*

straight a-capering; he will fence with his own shadow. If I should marry him, I should marry twenty husbands. If he would despise me, I would forgive him – for if he love me to madness, I shall never requite him.

NERISSA What say you then to Falconbridge, the young baron of England? 70

PORTIA You know I say nothing to him, for he understands not me, nor I him. He hath neither Latin, French nor Italian – and you will come into the court and swear that I have a poor pennyworth in the English. He is a proper man's picture – but alas, who can converse with a dumb-show? How oddly he is suited! I think he bought his doublet in Italy, his round hose in France, his bonnet in Germany, and his behaviour everywhere!

NERISSA What think you of the Scottish lord, his 80 neighbour?

PORTIA That he hath a neighbourly charity in him, for he borrowed a box of the ear of the Englishman and swore he would pay him again when he was able. I think the Frenchman became his surety and sealed under for another.

NERISSA How like you the young German, the Duke of Saxony's nephew?

PORTIA Very vilely in the morning, when he is sober – and most vilely in the afternoon, when he 90 is drunk. When he is best, he is a little worse than a man; and when he is worst, he is little better than a beast. And the worst fall that ever fell, I hope I shall make shift to go without him.

NERISSA If he should offer to choose, and choose the right casket, you should refuse to perform

[100] Rhenish   *white wine, supposedly stronger than red*

[109] by some other sort   *in some other way*
[110] imposition   *decree (in his will)*

[112] Sibylla   *a prophetess in classical legend; Apollo promised
her as many years of life as the grains of sand that she held in her hand*
[113] Diana   *goddess of hunting and symbol of virginity*
[114] parcel   *set*

[118] Do you not remember   *The inquiry is probably made
rather archly!*
[119–20] a scholar and a soldier   *In the sixteenth century this
combination was deemed ideal for a courtier.*

[122–3] as I think so was he called   *Perhaps Portia wants to
moderate the eagerness of her response (' Yes, yes . . .') with this show
of doubt!*

your father's will if you should refuse to accept
him.

PORTIA Therefore, for fear of the worst, I pray thee
set a deep glass of Rhenish wine on the contrary 100
casket, for if the devil be within and that
temptation without, I know he will choose it. I
will do anything, Nerissa, ere I will be married to
a sponge.

NERISSA You need not fear, lady, the having any of
these lords. They have acquainted me with their
determinations, which is indeed to return to their
home and to trouble you with no more suit,
unless you may be won by some other sort than
your father's imposition, depending on the 110
caskets.

PORTIA If I live to be as old as Sibylla, I will die as
chaste as Diana unless I be obtained by the
manner of my father's will. I am glad this parcel
of wooers are so reasonable, for there is not one
among them but I dote on his very absence; and
I pray God grant them a fair departure.

NERISSA Do you not remember, lady, in your
father's time, a Venetian — a scholar and a
soldier — that came hither in company of the 120
Marquis of Montferrat?

PORTIA Yes, yes, it was Bassanio — as I think so
was he called.

NERISSA True, madam. He, of all the men that ever
my foolish eyes looked upon, was the best
deserving a fair lady.

PORTIA I remember him well, and I remember him
worthy of thy praise.

[130] the four strangers *Shakespeare's miscount here – six suitors have just been under discussion – is not obvious in performance.*

[138] condition *character*
[138–9] complexion of a devil *a black skin*
[139] shrive me *hear my confession and absolve me (as the priest does)*

ACT ONE, scene 3

Another change of key – abruptly back from the radiant cheerfulness of Belmont to 'hard dealings', sly tactics and intense religious/racial malice in Venice.

Shylock *The name itself has an unlovely ring. It may derive from the Hebrew 'Shallach', meaning a cormorant, which was Elizabethan slang for a usurer. The components 'shy' and 'lock' strongly suggest the secret hoarding of the miser.*

[1] Three thousand ducats *A ducat was a Venetian gold piece. Three thousand of them amount to a huge sum – over £20 000 in today's money.*

[1,3,6] well *'I sée' – the repetition of the word ponderously confirming each element in the proposed loan, increases Bassanio's impatience – as Shylock intends it to.*

[7] stead me *supply me (with the money)*

Enter a SERVINGMAN

How now, what news?

SERVINGMAN The four strangers seek for you, 130
madam, to take their leave; and there is a fore-
runner come from a fifth, the Prince of Morocco,
who brings word the Prince his master will be
here tonight.

PORTIA If I could bid the fifth welcome with so
good heart as I can bid the other four farewell,
I should be glad of his approach. If he have the
condition of a saint and the complexion of a
devil, I had rather he should shrive me than wive
me. Come, Nerissa. Sirrah, go before. Whiles we 140
shut the gate upon one wooer, another knocks at
the door.

[Exeunt

Scene 3. *Enter* BASSANIO *with* SHYLOCK *the Jew*

SHYLOCK Three thousand ducats – well.

BASSANIO Ay sir, for three months.

SHYLOCK For three months – well.

BASSANIO For the which, as I told you, Antonio
shall be bound.

SHYLOCK Antonio shall become bound – well.

BASSANIO May you stead me? Will you pleasure me?
Shall I know your answer?

SHYLOCK Three thousand ducats for three months,
and Antonio bound. 10

BASSANIO Your answer to that?

SHYLOCK Antonio is a good man.

BASSANIO Have you heard any imputation to the
contrary?

THE MERCHANT OF VENICE

[16, 17] 'a good man'/he is sufficient (*Antonio is*) *a rich businessman* (*and so*)/*he is an adequate surety for the loan.* (*In Shylock's view Antonio is 'good' only financially, not morally.*)

[17] his means are in supposition *one may wonder how reliable his way of making money really is*

[18] argosy *a big trading ship*

[20] the Rialto *the Venetian Stock Exchange, a regular meeting-place for merchants. The bridge leading to it was often called 'the Rialto' too.*

[21] ventures *see I. 1. 15*

[22] squandered *lavishly scattered*

[25–6] the peril . . . rocks *compare I. 1. 31*

[29] Be assured you may *You certainly may.* (*Bassanio probably speaks sharply, irritated by Shylock's deliberations and by his apparent lack of confidence in Antonio's assets.*)

[30] I will be assured *I intend to be thoroughly satisfied.* (*Perhaps the chance of 'catching' Antonio through the bond has already entered Shylock's mind.*)

[34] pork *forbidden meat in the Jewish religion*

to eat . . . into *an allusion to Jesus' destruction of the Gadarene swine (Mark 5: 1–17).*

[36]. I will buy with you . . . *This sentence, like the scornful climax of the previous one, seems directed more at the Christian world (and so perhaps at the audience) than at Bassanio personally; in which case, 'you' includes Christians in general and Shylock moves to a stage-position suitable for his imminent 'aside'.*

[37–8] I will not eat . . . nor pray with you *This is not only the pride of the alien, asserting itself in a society to which he 'belongs' only in a business role. To an orthodox Jew eating and drinking are acts intimately connected with religion, like praying (and this makes Shylock's later decision to eat with the Christians 'in hate' (II. 5. 14) the more deplorable).*

[39–40] What news . . . comes here? *Seeing Antonio approach, Shylock pretends not to recognise him – a deliberate discourtesy. In 'cutting' him thus, Shylock, in a manner of speaking, gets his knife into Antonio from the moment the merchant appears.*

[42] fawning publican *This is Shylock's contemptuous comment on the warm and friendly way Antonio greets Bassanio – 'like a servile inn-keeper'.*

54

SHYLOCK Ho no, no, no, no! My meaning in saying
he is 'a good man' is to have you understand me
that he is sufficient. Yet his means are in supposition – he hath an argosy bound to Tripolis,
another to the Indies; I understand, moreover,
upon the Rialto, he hath a third at Mexico, a   20
fourth for England; and other ventures he hath
squandered abroad. But ships are but boards,
sailors but men; there be land-rats and water-
rats, water-thieves and land-thieves (I mean
pirates); and then there is the peril of waters,
winds and rocks. The man is, notwithstanding,
sufficient. Three thousand ducats – I think I may
take his bond.

BASSANIO Be assured you may.

SHYLOCK I will be assured I may: and that I may be   30
assured, I will bethink me. May I speak with
Antonio?

BASSANIO If it please you to dine with us.

SHYLOCK Yes, to smell pork, to eat of the habitation
which your prophet the Nazarite conjured the
devil into! I will buy with you, sell with you, talk
with you, walk with you, and so following; but I
will not eat with you, drink with you, nor pray
with you. What news on the Rialto? Who is he
comes here?   40

Enter ANTONIO

BASSANIO [*Going to meet him*] This is Signior
Antonio.

SHYLOCK [*Aside*] How like a fawning publican he
looks.
  I hate him for he is a Christian;

[44] low simplicity   *base and foolish plainness. Shylock despises Antonio's straight dealing (see ll. 51–2) and resents it as an interference with his own business as a moneylender.*

[45] gratis   *without taking interest on the repayment*

[46] usance   *a 'polite' term for usury (moneylending at extortionate interest rates)*

[47] upon the hip   *at a disadvantage. (From wrestling, the term describes a hold by which one can throw one's opponent to the ground.)*

[48–9] the ancient grudge . . . sacred nation   *Behind the hatred that Shylock and Antonio feel for each other lies the inherited weight of centuries of racial prejudice and religious bitterness.*

[49] rails   *pours angry abuse*

[51] my bargains, and my well-won thrift   *Innocuous terms describing his business success, the words 'whitewash' the hard dealing and exorbitant profit in Shylock's usury.*

[52] interest   *monetary gain; a less attractive name than 'thrift' (which has a suggestion of virtue about it)*

[56] the gross   *the full amount*

[61] Your worship   *Shylock is now extravagantly courteous – with a sly, taunting intention.*

the last . . . mouths   *we were just talking about you*

[62] albeit   *although*

[64] ripe wants   *pressing needs*

[65] possessed   *informed*

But more, for that in low simplicity
He lends out money gratis and brings down
The rate of usance here with us in Venice.
If I can catch him once upon the hip,
I will feed fat the ancient grudge I bear him.
He hates our sacred nation, and he rails –
Even there where merchants most do congre-
    gate –   50
On me, my bargains, and my well-won thrift,
Which he calls interest. Cursèd be my tribe
If I forgive him!
BASSANIO   Shylock, do you hear?
SHYLOCK [*Not facing them*] I am debating of my
    present store,
And by the near guess of my memory
I cannot instantly raise up the gross
Of full three thousand ducats. What of that?
Tubal, a wealthy Hebrew of my tribe,
Will furnish me. [*Turning to* BASSANIO] But
    soft, how many months
Do you desire? [*To* ANTONIO] Rest you fair,
    good signior!   60
Your worship was the last man in our mouths.
ANTONIO Shylock, albeit I neither lend nor borrow
By taking nor by giving of excess,
Yet to supply the ripe wants of my friend,
I'll break a custom. [*To* BASSANIO] Is he yet
    possessed
How much ye would?
SHYLOCK   Ay, ay, three thousand ducats.
ANTONIO And for three months.
SHYLOCK I had forgot – three months, [*To* BAS-
SANIO] you told me so.

57

[71] **Upon advantage**   *on terms involving interest*

[75] **the third possessor**   *Jacob's elder brother, Esau should have inherited from his father Isaac the possessions that Isaac inherited from his father Abraham, the founder of the Jewish race. Hence Esau would have been 'the third possessor'; but 'his wise mother', Rebekah, helped Jacob (her favourite son) to trick Esau out of his birthright and paternal blessing. The story is told in Genesis 25: 29–34 and Genesis 27 – and Shylock clearly approves of the double-dealing involved in it.*

[78] **Mark what Jacob did**   *Shylock now summarises the story of Jacob's sharp practice as a shepherd working for his uncle, Laban (as told in Genesis 30: 25–43), and remains very proud of his ancestor's craftiness in profit-making.*

[79] **were compromised**   *agreed*

[80] **eanlings**   *new-born lambs*
     streaked and pied   *with 'parti-coloured', spotted fleeces*

[81] **fall as Jacob's hire**   *count as Jacob's wages*
     rank   *on heat*

[85] **peeled me certain wands**   *tore off strips of bark from some sticks (so that they looked streaked with white)*

[87] **fulsome**   *fat*

[88] **eaning**   *lambing*

[89] **Fall**   *give birth to*

[90–1] **This . . . not**   *Compare [40]. Shylock implies that Jacob's way of 'thriving' (by not strictly stealing, but very nearly) was morally admirable and divinely approved, and that the 'thrift' of usury is comparably so.*

[92] **venture**   *risky enterprise*
     served   *was a servant*

[*To* ANTONIO] Well then, your bond. And let
me see – but hear you,

Methoughts you said you neither lend nor
borrow   70

Upon advantage.

ANTONIO   I do never use it.

SHYLOCK When Jacob grazed his uncle Laban's
sheep –

This Jacob from our holy Abram was

(As his wise mother wrought in his behalf)

The third possessor; ay, he was the third –

ANTONIO And what of him? Did he take interest?

SHYLOCK No, not take interest, not as you would say

Directly interest. Mark what Jacob did:

When Laban and himself were compromised

That all the eanlings which were streaked and
pied   80

Should fall as Jacob's hire, the ewes being
rank

In end of autumn turnèd to the rams;

And when the work of generation was

Between these woolly breeders in the act,

The skilful shepherd peeled me certain wands,

And in the doing of the deed of kind

He stuck them up before the fulsome ewes

Who, then conceiving, did in eaning time

Fall parti-coloured lambs, and those were
Jacob's.

This was a way to thrive, and he was blest;   90

And thrift is blessing if men steal it not.

ANTONIO This was a venture, sir, that Jacob served
for,

A thing not in his power to bring to pass,

[95] Was . . . good? *Did you bring up this story to justify usury?*

[97] I make it breed as fast *A smug jibe, full of 'falsehood' –
for Shylock's way of increasing his money ('a breed of barren metal',
l. 135) has nothing in common with natural propagation. (His
proposal for the bond will very shortly make the same false suggestion
that money-matters and living matter are equal in kind.)*

[103] O . . . hath *A common Shakespearean theme, this 'sentence' (compare Portia's in I. 2. 19) also epitomises one of the play's
major concerns.*

[105] the rate *i.e. 'at which I will charge you interest' – a mere
pretence, for the 'pound of flesh' idea is presumably in Shylock's mind
already*
[107] beholding *beholden; bound*

[108] rated *berated; scolded. Shylock's remark 'let me see the
rate' reminds him how sharply Antonio has 'rated' him in the past.
Now, with the merchant dependent on his services, he seizes the
chance to get his own back in his own sardonic fashion.*
[109] usances *see [46]*
[110] a patient shrug *A typical Jewish gesture.*
[111] sufferance *long-suffering; endurance*
    badge *particular characteristic*
[112] misbeliever *heretic (not an atheist 'unbeliever')*
[113] gaberdine *a long loose cloak*
[114] use of *both 'employing' and 'gaining interest on'*
[116] Go to, then *an expression of exasperation*
[118] void your rheum *spit*

But swayed and fashioned by the hand of
  heaven.
Was this inserted to make interest good?
Or is your gold and silver ewes and rams?

SHYLOCK I cannot tell; I make it breed as fast.
But note me, signior.

ANTONIO   Mark you this, Bassanio,
The devil can cite Scripture for his purpose.
An evil soul producing holy witness   100
Is like a villain with a smiling cheek,
A goodly apple rotten at the heart.
O what a goodly outside falsehood hath!

SHYLOCK Three thousand ducats – 'tis a good round
  sum.
Three months from twelve – then let me see
  the rate.

ANTONIO Well, Shylock, shall we be beholding to
  you?

SHYLOCK Signior Antonio, many a time and oft
In the Rialto you have rated me
About my moneys and my usances.
Still have I borne it with a patient shrug,   110
For sufferance is the badge of all our tribe.
You call me 'misbeliever', 'cut-throat dog',
And spit upon my Jewish gaberdine;
And all for use of that which is mine own.
Well then, it now appears you need my help.
Go to, then. You come to me, and you say,
'Shylock, we would have moneys'; you say so;
You that did void your rheum upon my beard
And foot me as you spurn a stranger cur
Over your threshold. Moneys is your suit.   120
What should I say to you? Should I not say,

[124] in a bondman's key   *on a slave's note*
[125] bated   *reduced*

[131-8] I . . . penalty   *This outburst is the most animated speech that Antonio makes in the entire play. He is quite unrepentant about the offence he has given to Shylock, but angered at having this offensive behaviour paraded with such zest before his friend Bassanio.*
[134-5] for . . . friend   *whoever heard of true friends taking interest on loans they make to each other?*

[137] Who   *from whom*

[139-40]   *With this cool lie Shylock leads his enemies on by combining surprise and reassurance in a single stroke – a calculated preliminary to the 'pound of flesh' proposal.*
[141] doit   *jot (also the name of a small Dutch coin)*

[143] kind   *a double sense – first (and falsely) 'benevolent' and then 'natural'*
[145] notary   *a clerk officially appointed to draw up contracts*
[146] single bond   *a simple agreement made with one person*
    in a merry sport   *Shylock completes his game with his enemy by seeming to offer the 'forfeit' as an agreeable substitute-arrangement for the 'usance' that Antonio objects to so much. (The Jew's skill at rigging things to his own desire seems quite as apt and cunning as his forefather Jacob's was.)*
[149] Expressed in the condition   *set down in the formal agreement*
[150] nominated for   *named as*
    equal pound   *an accurate, just weight*

'Hath a dog money? Is it possible
A cur can lend three thousand ducats?' Or
Shall I bend low, and in a bondman's key,
With bated breath and whispering humbleness,
Say this:
'Fair sir, you spat on me on Wednesday last;
You spurned me such a day; another time
You called me "dog" – and for these courtesies
I'll lend you thus much moneys'?   130

ANTONIO I am as like to call thee so again,
To spit on thee again, to spurn thee too.
If thou wilt lend this money, lend it not
As to thy friends – for when did friendship take
A breed of barren metal of his friend? –
But lend it rather to thine enemy,
Who, if he break, thou may'st with better face
Exact the penalty.

SHYLOCK   Why look you how you storm!
I would be friends with you and have your love,
Forget the shames that you have stained me
    with,   140
Supply your present wants, and take no doit
Of usance for my moneys, and you'll not hear
    me.
This is kind I offer.

BASSANIO This were kindness.

SHYLOCK   This kindness will I show.
Go with me to a notary; seal me there
Your single bond, and, in a merry sport,
If you repay me not on such a day,
In such a place, such sum or sums as are
Expressed in the condition, let the forfeit
Be nominated for an equal pound   150

63

THE MERCHANT OF VENICE

[151] fair flesh *Possibly implying that Shylock's skin is darker than the Venetian's.*

[154] kindness *natural friendliness (spoken ironically, no doubt)*

[156] dwell *remain*

[162–3] teaches . . . others *teach them to be suspicious of other people's propositions*

[164] break his day *fail to pay on the promised date*
[164–8] If . . . goats *The air of sweet reason in Shylock's question, and the literal truth of his own answer to it (for Antonio's flesh would be neither as valuable in itself nor as saleable as mutton, beef or goat-meat!) deflect attention from his murderous intent and give a scrap of polite cover to a sardonic insult.*

[173] And . . . straight *Shylock (or Shakespeare) seems to have forgotten the need to borrow from Tubal (see l. 56).*

[176] fearful *untrustworthy*
[177] knave *servant*
[179] The . . . kind *The remark (foreshadowing an outcome in Act Four) is more ironic than Antonio intends, for there has been precious little kindness – Christian or Hebrew – shown in this scene.*

    Of your fair flesh, to be cut off and taken
    In what part of your body pleaseth me.
ANTONIO Content, in faith. I'll seal to such a bond
    And say there is much kindness in the Jew.
BASSANIO You shall not seal to such a bond for me!
    I'll rather dwell in my necessity.
ANTONIO Why fear not, man; I will not forfeit it.
    Within these two months – that's a month
       before
    This bond expires – I do expect return
    Of thrice three times the value of this bond.   160
SHYLOCK O father Abram, what these Christians are,
    Whose own hard dealings teaches them suspect
    The thoughts of others! [*To* BASSANIO] Pray
       you tell me this –
    If he should break his day, what should I gain
    By the exaction of the forfeiture?
    A pound of man's flesh taken from a man
    Is not so estimable, profitable neither,
    As flesh of muttons, beefs or goats. I say
    To buy his favour I extend this friendship.
    If he will take it, so; if not, adieu.   170
    And for my love I pray you wrong me not.
ANTONIO Yes, Shylock, I will seal unto this bond.
SHYLOCK Then meet me forthwith at the notary's.
    Give him direction for this merry bond,
    And I will go and purse the ducats straight,
    See to my house, left in the fearful guard
    Of an unthrifty knave, and presently
    I'll be with you.   [*Exit*
ANTONIO   Hie thee, gentle Jew.
    The Hebrew will turn Christian; he grows
       kind.

BASSANIO I like not fair terms and a villain's
    mind.   180
ANTONIO Come on. In this there can be no dismay;
    My ships come home a month before the day.
                                    [Exeunt

THE MERCHANT OF VENICE

ACT TWO, scene 1

A short scene, keeping track of the situation at Belmont. After Antonio's undismayed confidence in the future, in the closing lines of I. 3, the dialogue here rings with reference to hazard: 'the lottery of my destiny', 'try my fortune', 'play at dice', 'blind Fortune', 'take your chance', 'my chance', 'your hazard'. And, with a bold fanfare, it presents another kind of confidence, that of the Prince of Morocco.

Prince of Morocco *Another alien in the play, but one of quite a different order from Shylock. He is dignified, noble and valiant, while being far too self-regarding. He does not talk to Portia so much as declaim in front of her his own status, his exploits and his worth. As 'a tawny Moor' his skin is dark-coloured but not black — and with his followers 'all in white' like himself ('accordingly') he and his train make a handsome, indeed dazzling, display.*

[2] **shadowed livery** *dark uniform (such as a king or great nobleman would give to his staff in Elizabethan times; see II. 2. 119)*
     burnished *brightly shining*
[3] **near bred** *Morocco means he has been brought up close to the sun, no doubt, but the phrase also carries a hint of a kinship with the Sun-god ('Phoebus' l. 5), in keeping with his fondness for extravagant personal assertion.*
[6] **make incision** *cut ourselves (a swaggering way to prove a point)*
[7] **reddest** *the redder your blood the greater your courage: a traditional notion*
[8] **aspect** *face*
[9] **feared the valiant** *made brave men quake*
[12] **to steal your thoughts** *as a way of securing your interest (in me)*
[14] **by nice direction** *by the specific guidance*
[16] **Bars . . . choosing** *prohibits me from making a free choice*
[17] **scanted** *limited*
[18] **hedged me by his wit** *constrained me in his wisdom*
[20] **stood as fair** *both 'had as good a chance' and 'seemed as light-skinned'*
[20-2] **Yourself . . . affection** *A somewhat mischievous compliment in the light of Portia's feelings about all her previous suitors, and of her opinion of Morocco at the end of her last scene (see I. 2. 114-16 and I. 2. 135-40).*

[24] **scimitar** *a short curved sword, broadest at the pointed end*
[25] **Sophy** *Emperor (Shah) of Persia*

ACT TWO

Scene 1. *Flourish of cornets. Enter the* PRINCE OF
MOROCCO (*a tawny Moor all in white*), *and three or
four followers accordingly, with* PORTIA, NERISSA,
and their train

MOROCCO Mislike me not for my complexion,
The shadowed livery of the burnished sun,
To whom I am a neighbour and near bred.
Bring me the fairest creature northward born,
Where Phoebus' fire scarce thaws the icicles,
And let us make incision for your love
To prove whose blood is reddest, his or mine.
I tell thee, lady, this aspèct of mine
Hath feared the valiant. By my love I swear,
The best-regarded virgins of our clime   10
Have loved it too. I would not change this hue,
Except to steal your thoughts, my gentle queen.
PORTIA In terms of choice I am not solely led
By nice direction of a maiden's eyes.
Besides, the lottery of my destiny
Bars me the right of voluntary choosing.
But if my father had not scanted me,
And hedged me by his wit to yield myself
His wife who wins me by that means I told you,
Yourself, renownèd Prince, then stood as fair   20
As any comer I have looked on yet
For my affection.
MOROCCO   Even for that I thank you.
Therefore I pray you lead me to the caskets
To try my fortune. By this scimitar
That slew the Sophy and a Persian prince

69

[26] Sultan Solyman *The Turkish Sultan had made war (unsuccessfully) against the Persians in 1535.*

[32] Lichas *Hercules' servant*

[33] Which is *i.e. to see which is. Fighting, not dicing, was Hercules' habitual way of proving himself to be 'the better man'.*

[31–8] But . . . grieving *It now occurs to Morocco that his bravery as a warrior will not help him at all in the 'lottery' of the caskets and momentarily he is dismayed ('alas the while') – most particularly (in his self-regarding way) by the thought of losing to a 'lesser' man than himself ('one unworthier').*

[35] Alcides *another name for Hercules*

[42] advised *careful*

[43] Nor will not *nor will I (ever ask anyone else to be my wife if I choose the wrong casket)*

[44] forward to the temple *where Morocco is to swear his oath*

ACT TWO, scene 2

Back to Venice: from the would-be sublime declarations of Morocco, in blank verse, to the wilfully ridiculous ones of Launcelot Gobbo, in prose.

Gobbo *A fitting name for a comedian! Like many clowns he makes much of his comic effect through the manner of his performance (in gestures, facial expressions, tone of voice, and so on). Like the more professional 'Fools', whom he tries to emulate, he relies a lot on proverbs, popular lore, common sayings. And he juggles industriously with words and meanings. But he sometimes mixes them up more foolishly than he realises. He entertains his audience; but a good Fool would have a sharper wit and more wisdom in making mocking commentary on human pretensions.*

[1] serve me *assist me. He has already decided to leave Shylock. His 'argument' on the subject is for entertainment only.*

[2–3] The fiend is at mine elbow . . . *He launches into a skit of a medieval morality play, in which characters such as Conscience and the Devil, representing good and evil, would try from opposite sides of the stage to win the soul of the character Man, in the middle. Though old-fashioned, such plays were still familiar to Elizabethans. Launcelot probably clowns about the stage, acting out all three roles during his speech.*

[4–5] Gobbo . . . Gobbo *For a moment he mimics the 'fiendish' formality and precision of legal language.*

That won three fields of Sultan Solyman,
I would o'erstare the sternest eyes that look,
Outbrave the heart most daring on the earth,
Pluck the young sucking cubs from the she-
bear,
Yea, mock the lion when he roars for prey,   30
To win thee, lady. But alas the while,
If Hercules and Lichas play at dice
Which is the better man, the greater throw
May turn by fortune from the weaker hand.
So is Alcides beaten by his page,
And so may I, blind Fortune leading me,
Miss that which one unworthier may attain,
And die with grieving.

PORTIA   You must take your chance,
And either not attempt to choose at all
Or swear before you choose, if you choose
wrong   40
Never to speak to lady afterward
In way of marriage. Therefore be advised.

MOROCCO Nor will not. Come, bring me unto my
chance.

PORTIA First, forward to the temple; after dinner
Your hazard shall be made.

MOROCCO   Good fortune then,
To make me blest or cursèd'st among men!
                    [*Flourish of cornets. Exeunt*

Scene 2. *Enter* LAUNCELOT GOBBO (*the clown*), *alone*

LAUNCELOT Certainly my conscience will serve me
to run from this Jew my master. The fiend is at
mine elbow and tempts me, saying to me, 'Gobbo,
Launcelot Gobbo, good Launcelot,' or 'Good

[10] with thy heels *utterly (the sort of obvious pun that Launce-lot relishes)*

[11] pack *hurry off*

Fia! *For 'Via!' – an Italian exhortation, such as one might use to a horse or a servant, meaning 'Away!'.*

[12] For the heavens *A very odd oath for the Devil to utter!*

[14] hanging about the neck of my heart *like a woman trying to keep her loved one from leaving her. Launcelot lays on a touch of 'style', in the pathetic vein, here.*

[16–18] honest woman's son . . . grow to *His father was not altogether an honest man, as Launcelot hints by saying that he had a certain flavour, a certain taint. (Hot milk was said to 'grow to' when it burned in the saucepan.) There may be some bawdy innuendo, since 'honest' can mean 'moral' in a sexual sense.*

[24, 26] God bless the mark/saving your reverence *Little apologies for his 'strong language' in harping on the Devil's name in front of the audience. The sense amounts to 'May I be forgiven for saying so'.*

[28] incarnation *Launcelot's error for 'incarnate', meaning 'in human shape'.*

[28–9] in my conscience *to speak completely sincerely*

[33] I will run *As he does so, he runs into Old Gobbo.*

Old Gobbo *This simple rustic character serves as the clown's 'stooge', and their scene together has much in common with a music hall turn or a pantomime routine, with much stage-business.*

Gobbo,' or 'Good Launcelot Gobbo – use your
legs, take the start, run away.' My conscience
says, 'No, take heed, honest Launcelot, take
heed, honest Gobbo,' or (as aforesaid) 'honest
Launcelot Gobbo – do not run, scorn running
with thy heels.' Well, the most courageous fiend   10
bids me pack. 'Fia!' says the fiend. 'Away!' says
the fiend. 'For the heavens, rouse up a brave
mind,' says the fiend, 'and run.' Well, my conscience hanging about the neck of my heart says
very wisely to me, 'My honest friend Launcelot,
being an honest man's son' – or rather an honest
woman's son, for indeed my father did something smack, something grow to; he had a kind of
taste – well, my conscience says, 'Launcelot,
budge not.' 'Budge,' says the fiend. 'Budge not,'   20
says my conscience. 'Conscience,' say I, 'you
counsel well.' 'Fiend,' say I, 'you counsel well.'
To be ruled by my conscience, I should stay with
the Jew my master who, God bless the mark, is a
kind of devil; and to run away from the Jew, I
should be ruled by the fiend who, saving your
reverence, is the devil himself. Certainly the Jew
is the very devil incarnation; and in my conscience, my conscience is but a kind of hard
conscience to offer to counsel me to stay with the   30
Jew. The fiend gives the more friendly counsel.
I will run, fiend; my heels are at your command-
ment; I will run.

Enter OLD GOBBO, *with a basket*

OLD GOBBO Master young man, you I pray you,
which is the way to Master Jew's?

[37] sand-blind *half-blind. A wholly sightless man would be 'stone-blind', so Launcelot's 'high-gravel-blind' means 'almost totally blind'.*

[38–9] I will try confusions *He seems to have no motive for bamboozling his father, unless it be to test the old man's feelings for his (long-lost?) son. In which case there may be a pun on 'try conclusions', meaning 'carry out an experiment'.*

[47] sonties *saints (in Old Gobbo's country dialect)*

[50] young Master Launcelot *Pleased at being mistaken for one of the gentry, Launcelot plays up to the idea of 'Master young gentleman'.*

[51–2] raise the waters *make him cry*

[54] No master, sir *The old man knows that his son, as a poor servant, would have no right to the gentleman's title of 'Master', so he won't hear of it. Launcelot's game begins to fall flat!*

[56] well to live *The phrase means 'well-to-do', so Old Gobbo unwittingly contradicts himself. He probably thinks it means something like 'in good health'.*

[57] 'a *he*

[61] ergo *'therefore' in Latin. Launcelot tries to make his case for 'mastership' more persuasive with a spot of 'learning'.*

[66] father *Here, he uses the word – as it was commonly employed – to mean simply 'old man' (and Old Gobbo sticks to this sense of it when Launcelot begins to use it otherwise, l. 75)*

[68] the Sisters Three *Another name for the Fates; when they cut the thread of a man's life, he died.*

74

LAUNCELOT [*Aside*] O heavens, this is my true-
begotten father who, being more than sand-blind,
high-gravel-blind, knows me not. I will try confusions with him.

OLD GOBBO Master young gentleman, I pray you   40
which is the way to Master Jew's?

LAUNCELOT Turn up on your right hand at the next
turning, but at the next turning of all, on your
left; marry, at the very next turning turn of no
hand, but turn down indirectly to the Jew's
house.

OLD GOBBO By God's sonties, 'twill be a hard way to
hit! Can you tell me whether one Launcelot that
dwells with him, dwell with him or no?

LAUNCELOT Talk you of young Master Launcelot?   50
[*Aside*] Mark me now; now will I raise the
waters. [*Aloud*] Talk you of young Master
Launcelot?

OLD GOBBO No master, sir, but a poor man's son.
His father, though I say't, is an honest exceeding
poor man and, God be thanked, well to live.

LAUNCELOT Well, let his father be what 'a will, we
talk of young Master Launcelot.

OLD GOBBO Your worship's friend, and Launcelot,
sir.   60

LAUNCELOT But I pray you, ergo old man, ergo I
beseech you, talk you of young Master Launcelot?

OLD GOBBO Of Launcelot, an't please your mastership.

LAUNCELOT Ergo, Master Launcelot. Talk not of
Master Launcelot, father, for the young gentleman, according to Fates and Destinies and such
odd sayings, the Sisters Three and such branches

THE MERCHANT OF VENICE

[71] Marry *An exclamation derived from the oath 'By the Virgin Mary'.*

[74] hovel-post *the main timber supporting a shack*
[74-5] Do you know me, father? *Having 'raised the waters', Launcelot intends now to abandon his game of 'confusion', but his father stays confused!*

[83-4] it is a wise father . . . child *An inversion of the old proverb 'It's a wise child that knows his own father'.*

[93-4] your boy that was . . . that shall be *Kneeling for blessing, as in church, Launcelot parodies (semi-blasphemously) a prayer-book form of words.*

[100] thou be Launcelot *Finally convinced of his son's identity, the old man switches to a more homely form of address.*
[101] Lord worshipped might he be *The equivalent of 'Good Heavens' or 'Goodness gracious' in today's usage.*

76

of learning, is indeed deceased, or as you would
say in plain terms, gone to heaven. 70

OLD GOBBO Marry, God forbid! The boy was the
very staff of my age, my very prop.

LAUNCELOT [*Aside*] Do I look like a cudgel or a
hovel-post, a staff or a prop? [*Aloud*] Do you
know me, father?

OLD GOBBO Alack the day, I know you not, young
gentleman, but I pray you tell me, is my boy –
God rest his soul – alive or dead?

LAUNCELOT Do you not know me, father?

OLD GOBBO Alack, sir, I am sand-blind! I know you 80
not.

LAUNCELOT Nay, indeed if you had your eyes you
might fail of the knowing me; it is a wise father
that knows his own child. Well, old man, I will
tell you news of your son. [*He kneels*] Give me
your blessing. Truth will come to light; murder
cannot be hid long – a man's son may, but in the
end truth will out.

OLD GOBBO Pray you, sir, stand up. I am sure you
are not Launcelot my boy. 90

LAUNCELOT Pray you let's have no more fooling
about it, but give me your blessing. I am
Launcelot, your boy that was, your son that is,
your child that shall be.

OLD GOBBO I cannot think you are my son.

LAUNCELOT I know not what I shall think of that;
but I am Launcelot, the Jew's man, and I am sure
Margery your wife is my mother.

OLD GOBBO Her name is Margery indeed! I'll be
.sworn, if thou be Launcelot thou art mine own 100
flesh and blood. Lord worshipped might he be,

[102] what a beard ... *The old man has probably wandered blindly round behind his kneeling son and, reaching out to bless him, touches the (long) hair at the back of Launcelot's head.*

[103] fill-horse *cart horse (that works in the 'fills' or shafts)*

[109] Lord, how art thou changed *By now Launcelot is standing up and facing his father, whose outstretched hand now encounters a quite different part of his anatomy.*

[110] agree *or, as we might say, 'get on'*

[110–11] a present *Hence Old Gobbo's basket.*

[112] for mine own part *as far as I am concerned*

[113] set up my rest *made up my mind (with a quibbling pun on 'rest' in the next phrase)*

[114, 122] a very Jew/I am a Jew *The term 'Jew' or 'a real ("very") Jew' could be – indeed, still is, at times – applied disparagingly to a mean, heartless person of any religion.*

[115] a halter *a hangman's noose*

[116–17] you may tell ... ribs *you can count my fingers by fitting them into the hollows between my ribs (that's how famished I am!)*

[118] Give me your present *give your present*

[119] rare *fine*
     liveries *uniforms (see II. 1. 2)*

[Enter Bassanio] *He is clearly getting ready to go to Belmont in style. The preparations include a feast for his friends and new uniforms for his servants, as it is his habit to spend borrowed money lavishly.*

what a beard hast thou got! Thou hast got more
hair on thy chin than Dobbin my fill-horse has
on his tail.

LAUNCELOT [*Rising*] It should seem then that
Dobbin's tail grows backward. I am sure he had
more hair of his tail than I have of my face when
I last saw him.

OLD GOBBO Lord, how art thou changed! How dost
thou and thy master agree? I have brought him a 110
present. How 'gree you now?

LAUNCELOT Well, well; but for mine own part, as I
have set up my rest to run away, so I will not rest
till I have run some ground. My master's a very
Jew. Give him a present? Give him a halter! I am
famished in his service; you may tell every finger
I have with my ribs. Father, I am glad you are
come. Give me your present to one Master Bassanio, who indeed gives rare new liveries. If I
serve not him, I will run as far as God has any 120
ground. O rare fortune, here comes the man! To
him, father, for I am a Jew if I serve the Jew any
longer.

Enter BASSANIO, *with* LEONARDO, *and two* SERVANTS

BASSANIO [*To one* SERVANT] You may do so, but let
it be so hasted that supper be ready at the
farthest by five of the clock. See these letters
delivered, put the liveries to making, and desire
Gratiano to come anon to my lodging.

[*Exit one* SERVANT

LAUNCELOT To him, father!

OLD GOBBO God bless your worship! 130

[131] Gramercy   *thank you (from the French 'grand merci')*

[133] Not a poor boy . . . *Anxious to impress, and objecting to both 'poor' and 'boy' in his father's introduction, Launcelot cuts in on his own account. A spate of mutual interruption, and comic blunders in the Gobbos' attempts at refined language, begins here. Bassanio is left flummoxed (l. 152).*

[135] infection   *for 'affection' – a warm inclination*

[141] scarce cater-cousins   *hardly good friends*

[143] having done me wrong   *Presumably by the alleged famishing!*

[144] frutify   *a near-miss for 'fructify' (which Launcelot supposes to mean the same as 'notify')*

[146] a dish of doves   *Probably several dead birds. The gift intended originally for Shylock was a delicacy for a city-dweller, but it is doubtless treated as a comic 'prop' here.*

[147] my suit is   *the favour I would ask is*

[148] impertinent   *for 'pertinent' – relevant*

[150] though old man, yet poor man   *Perhaps, in his haste, Launcelot says 'poor' where he means 'good'. (He is obviously trying to present his father to Bassanio in the best light he can.)*

[154] the very defect   *for 'the very effect' – the whole point*

[158] hath preferred thee   *has recommended you for a better job with me (see Shylock's remarks about this at II. 5. 45)*

preferment   *promotion*

[160] so poor a gentleman   *True enough! Bassanio's social status relies entirely on borrowed money.*

[161] The old proverb is very well parted . . . *The proverb in Launcelot's mind is 'The grace of God is near enough'. By 'parting' it he implies that Bassanio, as a Christian, has 'the grace of God' even without money of his own, whereas Shylock, with 'enough' wealth, has no grace, being a Jew.*

BASSANIO Gramercy. Wouldst thou aught with me?

OLD GOBBO Here's my son, sir, a poor boy—

LAUNCELOT Not a poor boy, sir, but the rich Jew's man, that would, sir, as my father shall specify—

OLD GOBBO He hath a great infection, sir, as one would say, to serve—

LAUNCELOT Indeed, the short and the long is, I serve the Jew, and have a desire, as my father shall specify—

OLD GOBBO His master and he, saving your wor- 140 ship's reverence, are scarce cater-cousins.

LAUNCELOT To be brief, the very truth is that the Jew, having done me wrong, doth cause me, as my father, being I hope an old man, shall frutify unto you—

OLD GOBBO I have here a dish of doves that I would bestow upon your worship, and my suit is—

LAUNCELOT In very brief, the suit is impertinent to myself, as your worship shall know by this honest old man, and though I say it, though old man, yet 150 poor man, my father.

BASSANIO One speak for both. What would you?

LAUNCELOT Serve you, sir.

OLD GOBBO That is the very defect of the matter, sir.

BASSANIO [To LAUNCELOT] I know thee well; thou hast obtained thy suit.
　　　Shylock thy master spoke with me this day,
　　　And hath preferred thee – if it be preferment
　　　To leave a rich Jew's service to become
　　　The follower of so poor a gentleman.　　160

LAUNCELOT The old proverb is very well parted between my master Shylock and you, sir. You have the grace of God, sir, and he hath enough.

[167] more guarded *with more braid on it (perhaps suggesting that Launcelot is to rise to the rank of Bassanio's 'official' Fool, and will wear the traditional uniform of one, the much-braided motley coat)*

[170] table *the central part of his palm, where Launcelot now begins to tell his own fortune.*

[172] Go to *An exclamation like 'Dash it!' – in mock disappointment at his 'simple line of life'.*

[175] a simple coming-in *a humble income (from the wedding dowries). Rather more bluntly than his new-found master, Launcelot sees marriage as a financial business!*

[175–6] to scape drowning *Possibly a punning way of saying 'to avoid going bankrupt'.*

[177] the edge of a feather bed *A feather bed has no edge – so he may mean that he will (e)scape danger to life and limb easily. There may also be some bawdy joke intended.*

[179] gear *business (either the good fortune he has just read in his palm or that of joining Bassanio's retinue)*

[182] bestowed *Presumably on board the ship for Belmont.*

BASSANIO Thou speak'st it well. [*To* OLD GOBBO] Go,
  father, with thy son.

  [*To* LAUNCELOT] Take leave of thy old master
    and inquire

  My lodging out. [*To* SERVANT] Give him a livery
  More guarded than his fellows'. See it done.

  [*Exit* SERVANT

LAUNCELOT Father, in. I cannot get a service, no, I
  have ne'er a tongue in my head! Well, [*Looking
  at his palm*] if any man in Italy have a fairer table 170
  which doth offer to swear upon a book – I shall
  have good fortune! Go to, here's a simple line of
  life. Here's a small trifle of wives. Alas, fifteen
  wives is nothing; eleven widows and nine maids
  is a simple coming-in for one man. And then to
  scape drowning thrice, and to be in peril of my
  life with the edge of a feather-bed! Here are
  simple scapes. Well, if Fortune be a woman, she's
  a good wench for this gear. Father, come. I'll
  take my leave of the Jew in the twinkling.   180

    [*Exeunt* LAUNCELOT *and* OLD GOBBO

BASSANIO [*Giving a list*] I pray thee, good Leonardo,
  think on this.

  These things being bought and orderly be-
    stowed,

  Return in haste, for I do feast tonight

  My best-esteemed acquaintance. Hie thee, go.

LEONARDO My best endeavours shall be done herein.

Enter GRATIANO, *meeting* LEONARDO *on his way*

GRATIANO Where's your master?
LEONARDO   Yonder, sir, he walks.

    [*Exit*

[188] I have suit to you   *I have a favour to ask*

[191] Why then you must   *The wry tone suggests that Bassanio would not have granted the favour so readily if he had asked first what it was!*

[192] rude   *Not so much 'insulting' (though Gratiano can certainly be so, see later, in Act Four) as 'coarse'.*

[193] Parts that become thee   *qualities that suit you*

[196] Something too liberal   *rather too freely. (Out of friendship Bassanio phrases his criticism mildly.)*

[197] To . . . modesty   *to damp down with a sprinkling of decorum*

[199] misconstered   *misjudged*

[201] put on a sober habit   . *both 'assume a solemn bearing' and 'dress in respectable clothes' (and, possibly, 'refrain from drinking too much')*

[202] but   *only*

[204] saying   *being said*

[205] Thus with my hat   *Some exaggerated gesture accompanies the words, to support Gratiano's mockery of puritanical manners.*

[206] the observance of civility   *the good manners that go with polite behaviour*

[207–8] Like one . . . grandam   *like someone who takes great care to keep up a serious appearance to impress his granny (lest she cut him out of her will!)*

[210] gauge   *judge*

GRATIANO Signior Bassanio!

BASSANIO   Gratiano!

GRATIANO I have suit to you.

BASSANIO   You have obtained it.

GRATIANO You must not deny me. I must go with
    you to Belmont.   190

BASSANIO Why then you must. But hear thee,
    Gratiano:
    Thou art too wild, too rude, and bold of voice –
    Parts that become thee happily enough
    And in such eyes as ours appear not faults;
    But where thou art not known, why there they
      show
    Something too liberal. Pray thee take pain
    To allay with some cold drops of modesty
    Thy skipping spirit, lest through thy wild be-
      haviour
    I be misconstered in the place I go to,
    And lose my hopes.

GRATIANO   Signior Bassanio, hear me: 200
    If I do not put on a sober habit,
    Talk with respect, and swear but now and then,
    Wear prayer-books in my pocket, look
      demurely –
    Nay more, while grace is saying hood mine eyes
    Thus with my hat, and sigh and say 'Amen' –
    Use all the observance of civility
    Like one well studied in a sad ostent
    To please his grandam, never trust me more.

BASSANIO Well, we shall see your bearing.

GRATIANO Nay, but I bar tonight. You shall not
    gauge me   210
    By what we do tonight.

[212–13] put on . . . mirth   both 'make us laugh as much as you can' and 'dress in extravagant party attire' (compare l. 201 above)
[214] purpose merriment   intend to enjoy themselves

This scene has been largely about the seeking and granting of favours ('suits'), and about making a good impression. It thus helps to establish 'kindness' and 'seeming' as central, related themes in the play. (Both remain to the fore in the next scene.)

ACT TWO, scene 3

Since most of the 'scenery' in the Elizabethan theatre was created by the actors' words, the scenes of a play could follow each other very smoothly and rapidly. The next four continue a linked sequence, begun in II. 2 and set in various parts of Venice. The particular locations are always made clear for the audience in the dialogue. Here, for instance, the first two lines show where the scene takes place – and who this new character, Jessica, is.

Shakespeare uses this brief scene (i) to introduce another strand in the plot (about love and money, like the main one), (ii) to gather pace in the play and (iii) to isolate Shylock further – for now his gentle (?) daughter is planning to run away from him.

[10] Adieu   French for 'Goodbye'. Launcelot probably pronounces it 'A-dew' – with punning reference to his 'tears'.
    exhibit   for 'inhibit'. He pretends to be too sad at leaving her to be able to talk, but manages a mock-gallant farewell nonetheless, since he is a 'merry devil'.
[11] pagan   Not strictly accurate, since Jessica is a Jewess, not a heathen.
[12] play the knave and get thee   win you for his wife through some shrewd trick. As go-between, Launcelot is 'in the know' about the lovers' plans.
[13–14] These foolish drops . . . spirit   Weeping gets the better of me
[16] heinous   hateful
[19] I am not to his manners   I am in no way tied to him in character
[20] this strife   the struggle between duty (to her father) and love (for Lorenzo). Partly because of the rhyme marking the end of the scene, she sounds quite unperturbed, as though scarcely giving 'this strife' a second thought. But presumably the elopement has been in mind for some time. Shakespeare is sketching in the situation in brisk, light strokes. To us Jessica's attitude may seem heartless but the Elizabethan audience is unlikely to have judged her intentions adversely here.

BASSANIO   No, that were pity.
 I would entreat you rather to put on
 Your boldest suit of mirth, for we have friends
 That purpose merriment. But fare you well;
 I have some business.
GRATIANO And I must to Lorenzo and the rest,
 But we will visit you at supper-time.

             [Exeunt

Scene 3. *Enter* JESSICA *and* LAUNCELOT

JESSICA I am sorry thou wilt leave my father so.
 Our house is hell, and thou, a merry devil,
 Didst rob it of some taste of tediousness.
 But fare thee well; there is a ducat for thee –
 And, Launcelot, soon at supper shalt thou see
 Lorenzo, who is thy new master's guest.
 Give him this letter; do it secretly.
 And so farewell. I would not have my father
 See me in talk with thee.
LAUNCELOT Adieu. Tears exhibit my tongue! Most 10
 beautiful pagan, most sweet Jew, if a Christian
 do not play the knave and get thee, I am much
 deceived. But adieu. These foolish drops do
 something drown my manly spirit: adieu!
JESSICA Farewell, good Launcelot.

          [Exit LAUNCELOT
 Alack, what heinous sin is it in me
 To be ashamed to be my father's child!
 But though I am a daughter to his blood,
 I am not to his manners. O Lorenzo,
 If thou keep promise, I shall end this strife, 20
 Become a Christian and thy loving wife!

              [Exit

ACT TWO, scene 4

The unfolding of the elopement plans in this scene seems some-
what thinly contrived in cold print; but in performance the
sense of hasty conversation and all-round bustle carries things
along convincingly.

[1–3] *Lorenzo is planning a masque (l. 22), a surprise 'happening'*
for the closing stages of Bassanio's feast. Traditionally, masquers
disguised themselves in fancy dress and masks. In a group, accom-
panied by music and torch-bearers, they would arrive at a social
gathering in an elaborately stylish ('quaintly ordered') way and join
the company in a formal dance.

[5] spoke us yet of   *made our arrangements for*

[8] We have two hours . . .   *He may be late for supper! (See*
II. 2. 126.)

[9] to furnish us   *to get everything ready*

[10, 11] An . . . signify   *Launcelot may be trying to deliver his*
letter 'secretly' (see II. 3, 7) by dressing up his language — only to
have Lorenzo 'give the game away' a moment later!

      an   *if*

      break up this   *open this letter (by breaking the seal on it)*

      seem to signify   *inform you*

[12] the hand   *the writing. (The word-play on 'fair hand' that*
follows is a thoroughly conventional piece of lover's imagery.)

[15] By your leave   *Excuse me. (He wants to be off on his next*
errand, now that Lorenzo has read Jessica's letter.)

[23] *The idea of making Jessica his torch-bearer seems to have*
occurred to him while reading her letter. It is not something that 'she
hath directed' in the letter.

Scene 4. *Enter* GRATIANO, LORENZO, SALERIO *and* SOLANIO

LORENZO Nay, we will slink away in supper-time,
        Disguise us at my lodging, and return
        All in an hour.

GRATIANO We have not made good preparation.

SALERIO We have not spoke us yet of torch-bearers.

SOLANIO 'Tis vile, unless it may be quaintly ordered,
        And better in my mind not undertook.

LORENZO 'Tis now but four of clock. We have two
        hours
        To furnish us.

                Enter LAUNCELOT, *with a letter*

                Friend Launcelot, what's the news?

LAUNCELOT An it shall please you to break up this,   10
        it shall seem to signify.

LORENZO I know the hand. In faith, 'tis a fair hand,
        And whiter than the paper it writ on
        Is the fair hand that writ.

GRATIANO   Love-news, in faith!

LAUNCELOT By your leave, sir.

LORENZO Whither goest thou?

LAUNCELOT Marry, sir, to bid my old master the
        Jew to sup tonight with my new master the
        Christian.

LORENZO Hold here, take this. [*Gives money*] Tell
        gentle Jessica   20
        I will not fail her. Speak it privately.

                                [*Exit* LAUNCELOT
        [*To* SALERIO *and* SOLANIO] Go, gentlemen;
        Will you prepare you for this masque tonight?
        I am provided of a torch-bearer.

[30–3] I . . . readiness   *A rather obvious way of keeping the plot clear for the audience.*

[35] gentle daughter   *A pun on 'Gentile' may be intended, since she will become a Gentile on marriage.*

[36] And . . . foot   *Misfortune will never dare to cross her path*

[37] she   *Misfortune*
under this excuse   *for this reason*

[38] she   *Jessica*
issue to   *child of*
faithless   *Lorenzo clearly considers a non-Christian religion to be no faith at all – a widely held prejudice (see, for instance, Launcelot's term for Jessica: 'most beautiful pagan', II. 3. 10).*

[39] this   *the letter from Jessica*

ACT TWO, scene 5

Shylock has been a lurking presence in the dialogue of all the Venice scenes since we last saw him. Now, suddenly, 'the Jew' returns in person, on his home ground and very compelling.

[3] gormandise   *over-eat (though Launcelot considered himself 'famished', II. 1. 116)*

[5] rend apparel out   *wear holes in your clothes*

SALERIO Ay merry, I'll be gone about it straight.
SOLANIO And so will I.
LORENZO   Meet me and Gratiano
    At Gratiano's lodging some hour hence.
SALERIO 'Tis good we do so.
                         [*Exeunt* SALERIO *and* SOLANIO
GRATIANO Was not that letter from fair Jessica?
LORENZO I must needs tell thee all. She hath
    directed   30
    How I shall take her from her father's house,
    What gold and jewels she is furnished with,
    What page's suit she hath in readiness.
    If e'er the Jew her father come to heaven,
    It will be for his gentle daughter's sake;
    And never dare Misfortune cross her foot,
    Unless she do it under this excuse,
    That she is issue to a faithless Jew.
    Come, go with me; peruse this as thou goest.
    Fair Jessica shall be my torch-bearer.   40
                                              [*Exeunt*

Scene 5. *Enter* SHYLOCK, *with his former servant,*
LAUNCELOT

SHYLOCK Well, thou shalt see, thy eyes shall be thy
    judge,
    The difference of old Shylock and Bassanio –
    [*Calling* JESSICA] What, Jessica! – Thou shalt
    not gormandise
    As thou hast done with me – [*Calling again*]
    What, Jessica! –
    And sleep, and snore, and rend apparel out –
    [*Calling again*] Why, Jessica, I say!

[8] Your worship . . . bidding *Shylock often complained that his servant could do nothing without being told to. Now Launcelot cheekily implies that he has done nothing (wrong), since Shylock did not tell him to call out to Jessica.*

[14–15] But yet . . . Christian *He changes his mind about dining with Christians (see I. 3. 34–9) out of sheer spite, which is all the more alarming to observe because it erupts in the middle of cool judgement (as he says, the Christians do flatter him, and 'prodigal' is a very apt description of Bassanio). There is surely 'some ill a-brewing' for someone in this state.*

[18] For . . . tonight *This superstitious streak in the man is almost laughable. It momentarily evokes a farcical, pantomime miser.*

[20] reproach *Launcelot means 'approach', but Shylock sardonically takes him literally, for he expects to give and take offence among his Christian hosts.*

[22] they have conspired together *they have made special arrangements (for the masque)*

[22–7] I will not . . . afternoon *Launcelot mocks at Shylock's superstitious notions, by reeling off a garbled piece of nonsense full of seeming 'omens'. Black Monday was a name for Easter Monday.*

[30] the wry-necked fife *The fife is a small pipe, played with the head turned to one side.*

[31] casements *windows*

[32] the public street *Masquers often paraded through the streets on the way to their revelry.*

[33] with varnished faces *wearing masks (or lurid make-up)*

LAUNCELOT [*Calling too*]   Why, Jessica!
SHYLOCK Who bids thee call? I do not bid thee call.
LAUNCELOT Your worship was wont to tell me I
could do nothing without bidding.

Enter JESSICA

JESSICA Call you? What is your will?   10
SHYLOCK I am bid forth to supper, Jessica.
    There are my keys. But wherefore should I go?
    I am not bid for love – they flatter me;
    But yet I'll go in hate to feed upon
    The prodigal Christian. Jessica my girl,
    Look to my house. I am right loath to go.
    There is some ill a-brewing towards my rest,
    For I did dream of money bags tonight.
LAUNCELOT I beseech you, sir, go. My young master
doth expect your reproach.   20
SHYLOCK So do I his.
LAUNCELOT And they have conspired together. I will
not say you shall see a masque, but if you do,
then it was not for nothing that my nose fell a-
bleeding on Black Monday last at six o'clock
i'th'morning, falling out that year on Ash
Wednesday was four year in th'afternoon.
SHYLOCK What, are there masques? Hear you me,
    Jessica:
    Lock up my doors; and when you hear the
      drum
    And the vile squealing of the wry-necked fife, 30
    Clamber not you up to the casements then,
    Nor thrust your head into the public street
    To gaze on Christian fools with varnished
      faces;

[34] stop my house's ears   *close the shutters over the windows*

[35] shallow foppery   *empty foolishness. Such a doggedly spoil-sport attitude is faintly ridiculous. It must also be one of the things that make the house 'hell' for Jessica (II. 3, 2).*

[41–2] There will come . . . eye   *In this pointed jingle Launcelot carries out Lorenzo's instructions (II. 4. 20–1) and pays him a punning compliment in his absence. ('Dear as a Jew's eye' was a common way of saying that something was very precious.)*

[43] fool of Hagar's offspring   *Hagar, the Egyptian maid to Abraham's wife, bore him a son called Ishmael (Genesis 16). Abraham later rejected the boy (Genesis 21: 9–21). Shylock ironically identifies his 'outcast' servant with Ishmael.*

[45] patch   *fool*
    huge feeder   *see l.3 and II. 2. 115–17*

[46] in profit   *in growing proficient at his work (thereby increasing his usefulness to his employer)*

[47] wild-cat   *which is awake, and on the prowl, for most of the night*

    Drones . . . me   *I won't support idle creatures*

[48] and part with him . . . purse   *Again Shylock's tone seems to harden abruptly, from the musing, almost paternal note of his comments on Launcelot to gloating malice towards the Christian Bassanio.*

[53] fast . . . fast   *tight . . . quickly. ('He who keeps a tight hold on what he has got, soon prospers.')*

[55] if my fortune be not crossed   *if all goes well*
The scene closes down with Jessica's rhymed couplet 'answering back her father's. As she says her last line she probably draws closed in front of herself the curtains of the inner stage (with a visual pun on 'daughter, lost'), there to make a quick change into her page's suit before appearing on the balcony in the next scene.

But stop my house's ears, I mean my case-
    ments;
Let not the sound of shallow foppery enter
My sober house. By Jacob's staff I swear
I have no mind of feasting forth tonight;
But I will go. Go you before me, sirrah.
Say I will come.

LAUNCELOT   I will go before, sir.
    [*Aside to* JESSICA] Mistress, look out at window
    for all this –   40
    There will come a Christian by
    Will be worth a Jewess' eye.   [*Exit*

SHYLOCK What says that fool of Hagar's offspring,
    ha?

JESSICA His words were 'Farewell, mistress' –
    nothing else.

SHYLOCK The patch is kind enough, but a huge
    feeder,
Snail-slow in profit, and he sleeps by day
More than the wild-cat. Drones hive not with
    me;
Therefore I part with him – and part with him
To one that I would have him help to waste
His borrowed purse. Well, Jessica, go in.   50
Perhaps I will return immediately.
Do as I bid you; shut doors after you.
'Fast bind, fast find' –
A proverb never stale in thrifty mind.   [*Exit*

JESSICA Farewell; and if my fortune be not crossed,
    I have a father, you a daughter, lost.
                          [*Exit*

ACT TWO, scene 6

Until Antonio arrives, this scene has a gay, festive air, with the characters in fancy dress and perhaps accompanied by music. This atmosphere disguises, but does not wholly obscure, the fact that Jessica's 'kindness' to Lorenzo, in stealing away with her own 'dowry', is unkindness to her father. Her elopement is a 'seeming' game; and it is also a betrayal of religious and family bonds.

[1–2] This is the penthouse . . . stand *In II. 4 they were to meet at 'Gratiano's lodging'. Apparently Lorenzo has made this further arrangement with Gratiano and Salerio since we last saw them. The stage roof serves to suggest the porch ('penthouse') of Shylock's house.*

[4] lovers . . . clock *lovers are always ahead of time (at a rendezvous)*

[5–7] O . . . unforfeited *Love is celebrated much more eagerly at the betrothal stage than in a long-established marriage!*

[5] Venus' pigeons *the doves that draw the chariot of the goddess of love (or perhaps the term is simply a way of saying 'lovers')*

[8] That ever holds *That is always the case*

[9] keen appetite *Gratiano probably has the physical 'appetite' of Love in mind, as well as Bassanio's supper!*

[10–11] untread . . . measures *repeat for the umpteenth time his training exercises*

[11] unbated *unabated, undiminished*

[12–13] All things . . . enjoyed *A somewhat cynical philosophy that sums up a lot in Gratiano's character.*

[14] younger *a younger son (like the Prodigal Son in the parable – Luke 15: 11–32)*

prodigal *a wastrel spendthrift*

[15] scarfèd bark *a ship that sets off all dressed up with flags and bunting (like the dandified prodigal)*

[16, 19] the strumpet wind *Just as the prostitutes in the parable (Luke 15: 30) wasted the Prodigal Son's substance, so the capricious wind wears out the ship.*

[18] over-weathered ribs *the weather-beaten ship's main timbers (which stand out like the beggared prodigal's ribs)*

[14–19] *These lines, coming so soon after Shylock's reference to 'the prodigal Christian' (II. 5. 15), keep Bassanio's imminent venture to Belmont in the audience's mind, in a somewhat ominous light; and they offer another reminder (compare I. 1. 17–24 and I. 3. 25–6) of the rigours faced by Antonio's trading ships (his 'ventures').*

[21] abode *delay*

Scene 6. *Enter the masquers,* GRATIANO *and* SALERIO

GRATIANO This is the penthouse under which Lorenzo
 Desired us to make stand.

SALERIO   His hour is almost past.

GRATIANO And it is marvel he outdwells his hour,
 For lovers ever run before the clock.

SALERIO O ten times faster Venus' pigeons fly
 To seal love's bonds new-made, than they are wont
 To keep obligèd faith unforfeited!

GRATIANO That ever holds. Who riseth from a feast
 With that keen appetite that he sits down?
 Where is the horse that doth untread again 10
 His tedious measures with the unbated fire
 That he did pace them first? All things that are
 Are with more spirit chasèd than enjoyed.
 How like a younger or a prodigal
 The scarfèd bark puts from her native bay,
 Hugged and embracèd by the strumpet wind:
 How like the prodigal doth she return,
 With over-weathered ribs and ragged sails,
 Lean, rent, and beggared by the strumpet wind!

Enter LORENZO

SALERIO Here comes Lorenzo; more of this hereafter. 20

LORENZO Sweet friends, your patience for my long abode.
 Not I but my affairs have made you wait.
 When you shall please to play the thieves for wives,

[24] Approach *They all draw nearer to the balcony where Jessica will appear (from behind the closed curtains, probably).*

[26] Who are you? *She needs to ask because (i) Lorenzo is disguised and (ii) ''tis night'.*

[27] Albeit *although*

[31] yours *your love indeed. (Her question is a token gesture of 'Do you really love me only?' before she gives him the money.)*

[33] catch this casket *Like Bassanio's winning casket, later, it brings him wealth as well as a wife.*

[34–45] *No doubt Shakespeare's audience found Jessica's protestations more humorous than we do, since her part, like every feminine role in the play, was acted by a boy.*

[35] exchange *of clothes*

[41] What . . . shames *'Must I actually help to reveal my embarrassment (at wearing these clothes)?' She was expecting to be Lorenzo's page, but not his torch-bearer.*

[42] light *both 'apparent' and (spoken ironically) 'wanton'*

[43] an office of discovery *a torch-bearer's job is to throw light on things*

[44] obscured *kept hidden*

[45] garnish *costume*

[47] For . . . runaway *for the night that keeps our secret is slipping away fast (or possibly 'for the dark night is on our side, being ideal for eloping')*

[49] gild *overlay with gold. (She means to imply that she will then be even more attractive and 'valuable', and the zestful excess of the idea seems to impress Gratiano strongly.)*

I'll watch as long for you then. Approach –
Here dwells my father Jew. Ho! Who's within?

Enter JESSICA, *above, in boy's clothes*

JESSICA Who are you? Tell me for more certainty,
    Albeit I'll swear that I do know your tongue.
LORENZO Lorenzo, and thy love.
JESSICA Lorenzo certain, and my love indeed,
    For who love I so much? And now who knows   30
    But you, Lorenzo, whether I am yours?
LORENZO Heaven and thy thoughts are witness that
    thou art.
JESSICA Here, catch this casket; it is worth the pains.
    I am glad 'tis night, you do not look on me,
    For I am much ashamed of my exchange.
    But love is blind, and lovers cannot see
    The pretty follies that themselves commit;
    For if they could, Cupid himself would blush
    To see me thus transformèd to a boy.
LORENZO Descend, for you must be my torch-bearer. 40
JESSICA What, must I hold a candle to my shames?
    They in themselves, good sooth, are too too
      light.
    Why, 'tis an office of discovery, love,
    And I should be obscured.
LORENZO   So are you, sweet,
    Even in the lovely garnish of a boy.
    But come at once,
    For the close night doth play the runaway,
    And we are stayed for at Bassanio's feast.
JESSICA I will make fast the doors and gild myself
    With some more ducats, and be with you
      straight.   *[Exit above* 50

THE MERCHANT OF VENICE

[51] Now by my hood *An emphatic little phrase, equivalent to 'Well, I do declare'.*

a gentle *a noble lady (and, indeed, a Gentile)*

[52] Beshrew me but *A light oath, amounting to 'May woe befall me if it's not true that . . .'.*

[53–7] For . . . soul *Lorenzo's cumulative compliment gives Jessica time to descend from the balcony off-stage. In a romantic young lover such courtly, polished expression would be considered 'good form' – as would the biased view of the lady's wisdom, beauty and truth.*

[59] Our . . . stay *Presumably their friends are waiting, as arranged in II. 4 at Gratiano's lodging.*

[63] 'Tis nine o'clock *This time is impossible in theory but convincing in performance (see II. 4. 8 and 26 and, in this scene, ll. 2 and 3).*

[64] The wind is come about *The sudden change of wind turns the thoughts of the audience towards Belmont in readiness for the next scene.*

ACT TWO, scene 7

The opening fanfare – Morocco's signature-tune from II. 1 – shifts the action at a stroke from one casket scene to another, from the hustle and bustle in Venice to the air of ceremony at Belmont. Portia and Morocco, with their attendants, probably enter simultaneously and formally at opposite sides of the main stage. The words of the script continue to indicate the essential stage directions. They suggest, as the scene opens, that 'the several caskets' have been set up behind the closed curtains of the inner stage during II. 6.

[1] [To a servant] *The servant whom Portia addresses may well be Nerissa.*

discover *reveal*

[2] several *separate (the caskets are probably arranged on three individual stands)*

[4] *Morocco doubtless moves upstage of the caskets at this point, so as to be facing his hostess and the audience while he makes his choice.*

GRATIANO Now by my hood, a gentle and no Jew!
LORENZO Beshrew me but I love her heartily –
    For she is wise, if I can judge of her,
    And fair she is, if that mine eyes be true,
    And true she is, as she hath proved herself;·
    And therefore, like herself, wise, fair, and true,
    Shall she be placèd in my constant soul.

Enter JESSICA, *below*

What, art thou come? On, gentlemen, away!
Our masquing mates by this time for us stay.
      [*Exeunt* LORENZO, JESSICA *and* SALERIO

Enter ANTONIO, *as* GRATIANO *is leaving*

ANTONIO Who's there?   60
GRATIANO Signior Antonio?
ANTONIO Fie, fie, Gratiano, where are all the rest?
    'Tis nine o'clock; our friends all stay for you.
    No masque tonight. The wind is come about;
    Bassanio presently will go aboard.
    I have sent twenty out to seek for you.
GRATIANO I am glad on't. I desire no more delight
    Than to be under sail and gone tonight.
              [*Exeunt*

Scene 7. *Flourish of cornets. Enter* PORTIA, *with the*
PRINCE OF MOROCCO, *and both their trains*

PORTIA [*To a* SERVANT] Go, draw aside the curtains
    and discover
The several caskets to this noble Prince.
[*To* MOROCCO] Now make your choice.
MOROCCO This first, of gold, who this inscription
    bears –

[5, 7, 9] shall gain . . . shall get . . . must give *The inscriptions on the first two caskets are a verbal temptation to the reader's personal greed, supporting the visible and tactile one of their appearance.*

[8] This . . . blunt – *The warning on this third casket is as plainly unattractive as the metal it is made of –*

[10–12] How . . . withal *The dual suggestion of a gambling game (a kind of 'Find the Lady' or 'Winner Take All') and of a holy occasion (compare l. 40) fills the scene, making it peculiarly engaging.*

[14] back again *in reverse order*

[19] fair advantages *making a good profit*

[20] A golden . . . dross *A really refined person does not lower himself so far as to linger over shoddy things. (Lead is a 'base', non-precious metal).*

[22] virgin hue *whitish colour, the colour of innocence and chastity*

[25] with an even hand *steadily, as when hoping to balance scales*

[26–30] If . . . myself *To judge by your own opinion of yourself, you are full of merit, but even such a rating may not be good enough to win you Portia as your wife. However, to be daunted by such a thought would be sheer feebleness – not like you at all.*

'Who chooseth me shall gain what many men
    desire.'
The second, silver, which this promise carries –
'Who chooseth me shall get as much as he de-
    serves.'
This third, dull lead, with warning all as blunt –
'Who chooseth me must give and hazard all he
    hath.'
How shall I know if I do choose the right?   10
PORTIA The one of them contains my picture,
    Prince.
If you choose that, then I am yours withal.
MOROCCO Some god direct my judgement! Let me
    see –
I will survey the inscriptions back again.
What says this leaden casket?
'Who chooseth me must give and hazard all he
    hath.'
Must give – for what? For lead? Hazard for
    lead?
This casket threatens! Men that hazard all
Do it in hope of fair advantages.
A golden mind stoops not to shows of dross;   20
I'll then nor give nor hazard aught for lead.
What says the silver with her virgin hue?
'Who chooseth me shall get as much as he
    deserves.'
As much as he deserves? Pause there, Morocco,
And weigh thy value with an even hand.
If thou be'st rated by thy estimation,
Thou dost deserve enough, and yet 'enough'
May not extend so far as to the lady;
And yet to be afear'd of my deserving

[36] graved *engraved (with some dramatic irony in the hint of 'the grave', the outcome of his choice being what it is: l. 63)*

[38–47] *These lines are worth comparing, for their similarity in ideas and resonance, with Bassanio's account of Portia in I. 1. Extravagant compliment was 'the done thing' for a courtly lover, and equating his romantic devotion to his lady with the worship of a saint was a fairly standard ploy.*

[39] the four corners *the round earth's imagined corners – north, south, east and west*

[40] shrine *the image of a saint in a holy place of pilgrimage*
     mortal *living. Morocco over-stretches the compliment!*

[41] Hyrcanian deserts *Here be tigers! A wild region south of the Caspian Sea.*

[42] are as throughfares now *seem like main roads now*

[44–5] The watery . . . heaven *A somewhat overblown image of the stormy sea tossing spray at the sky, as if annoyed at not being able to reach it.*

[46] foreign spirits *suitors from overseas – with a punning reference to the belief that 'spirits' of the ghostly kind could not cross water easily*

[50–51] it were . . . cerecloth *lead would be too base and crude a metal to contain her corpse in its waxed shroud. (The dead bodies of well-to-do people were often embalmed and cased in lead for burial, instead of being coffined.)*

[52] immured *shut up*

[52–9] Or . . . within *Morocco's praise of the lady has degenerated into financial calculation. This equation of her worth as a person with 'worth' in money-values leads him to his downfall (see II. 9. 80–1).*

[56] angel *Known as an 'angel', this coin had roughly the same value as a ducat.*

[57] insculped upon *engraved on the coin's surface*

Were but a weak disabling of myself.   30
As much as I deserve? Why that's the lady!
I do in birth deserve her, and in fortunes,
In graces, and in qualities of breeding;
But more than these, in love I do deserve.
What if I strayed no farther, but chose here?
Let's see once more this saying graved in
    gold –
'Who chooseth me shall gain what many men
    desire.'
Why that's the lady! All the world desires her;
From the four corners of the earth they come
To kiss this shrine, this mortal breathing saint.   40
The Hyrcanian deserts and the vasty wilds
Of wide Arabia are as throughfares now
For princes to come view fair Portia.
The watery kingdom, whose ambitious head
Spits in the face of heaven, is no bar
To stop the foreign spirits, but they come
As o'er a brook to see fair Portia.
One of these three contains her heavenly
    picture.
Is't like that lead contains her? 'Twere damna-
    tion
To think so base a thought; it were too gross   50
To rib her cerecloth in the obscure grave.
Or shall I think in silver she's immured,
Being ten times undervalued to tried gold?
O sinful thought! Never so rich a gem
Was set in worse than gold. They have in
    England
A coin that bears the figure of an angel
Stampèd in gold, but that's insculped upon;

[61–2] There . . . yours *Portia's calm (even relieved?) response to his excitement suggests that she knows already that he has chosen wrongly.*

　　　my form　*my image*

[63] a carrion Death　*a skull. Morocco's choice is a 'sudden death', of a sort – it punctures his image of himself, and it condemns him to a bachelor life. The scroll's 'answer' to him is appropriate enough, but it is less obvious how the* skull *answers to the* inscription *on the gold casket, since very few men actually desire Death (as opposed to the many who desire gold).*

[67–8] Many . . . behold　*Many men have ruined, even lost, their lives because they were led astray by the sight of gold.*

[69] worms　*the worms that feed on the decomposing corpses*

[73] your suit is cold　*A common saying, meaning 'your hopes are dead'.*

[75] welcome frost　*He puts a brave face on things by rhyming in the doggerel metre of the verses he has just read, while wryly acknowledging that the rest of his days will lack the comforting warmth of a wife.*

[77] Thus losers part　*No fanfare, no rhetoric – a complete contrast to his arrival.*

[78] A gentle riddance　*He lost, and left, like a gentleman.*

　　　Draw the curtains　*Thus hidden, the caskets will remain in place on the inner stage, ready for II. 9.*

But here an angel in a golden bed
Lies all within. Deliver me the key.
Here do I choose, and thrive I as I may!   60
PORTIA There, take it, Prince; and if my form lie there,
        Then I am yours.

He opens the golden casket

MOROCCO   O hell! What have we here?
        A carrion Death, within whose empty eye
        There is a written scroll. I'll read the writing.
        'All that glisters is not gold –
        Often have you heard that told.
        Many a man his life hath sold
        But my outside to behold.
        Gilded tombs do worms infold.
        Had you been as wise as bold,   70
        Young in limbs, in judgement old,
        Your answer had not been inscrolled.
        Fare you well, your suit is cold.'
        [*Aside*] Cold indeed, and labour lost.
        Then farewell heat, and welcome frost.
        Portia, adieu. I have too grieved a heart
        To take a tedious leave. Thus losers part.
                                        [*Exit with his train*
PORTIA A gentle riddance. [*To* SERVANT] Draw the curtains, go.
        Let all of his complexion choose me so.
                                        [*Exeunt*

ACT TWO, scene 8

Back to Venice, to hear in quick succession of two more 'losers' – Shylock and Antonio. Through the device of reported action, the audience watches two small scenes within this one – and the difference in the Venetians' attitudes to the distress of 'the villain Jew' and to the distress of their merchant friend offers a discomforting contrast.

[4] raised *roused up, presumably from sleep. Shylock takes his trouble straight to the man at the top of Venetian law and order.*

[10] certified *assured, convinced*

[12] a passion *an emotional outcry*

[13] outrageous *full of sound and fury and bitter indignation*

   variable *Because Shylock's outcry mixed (or 'confused') various kinds of concern – for the loss of his daughter, for the loss of his ducats, and for punishment for those who have hurt him.*

[15-22] *Solanio accompanies these lines with a mocking imitation of the distraught Jew – a spectacle that Salerio finds vastly more amusing than most audiences do.*

[19] double ducats *coins of twice the normal value*

[20] two stones *Doubtless Solanio and Salerio share a snigger at a bawdy pun here, since 'stones' meant 'testicles' as well as 'gems'.*

[25] look he keep his day *see that he pays his bond by the appointed day*

[26] Or ... this *This thought introduces the second scene-within-the-scene with a distinct change of tone, from hilarity to (Antonio's) sadness.*

Scene 8. *Enter* SALERIO *and* SOLANIO

SALERIO Why, man, I saw Bassanio under sail;
With him is Gratiano gone along,
And in their ship I am sure Lorenzo is not.

SOLANIO The villain Jew with outcries raised the
Duke,
Who went with him to search Bassanio's
ship.

SALERIO He came too late, the ship was under sail,
But there the Duke was given to understand
That in a gondola were seen together
Lorenzo and his amorous Jessica.
Besides, Antonio certified the Duke   10
They were not with Bassanio in his ship.

SOLANIO I never heard a passion so confused,
So strange, outrageous, and so variable,
As the dog Jew did utter in the streets –
'My daughter! O my ducats! O my daughter!
Fled with a Christian! O my Christian ducats!
Justice! The law! My ducats and my daughter!
A sealèd bag, two sealèd bags of ducats,
Of double ducats, stol'n from me by my
daughter!
And jewels, two stones, two rich and precious
stones,   20
Stol'n by my daughter! Justice! Find the girl!
She hath the stones upon her, and the ducats!'

SALERIO Why, all the boys in Venice follow him,
Crying his stones, his daughter, and his ducats.

SOLANIO Let good Antonio look he keep his day,
Or he shall pay for this.

SALERIO   Marry, well remembered.

THE MERCHANT OF VENICE

[27] reasoned *made conversation*

[28] the narrow seas *the English Channel*

[29] miscarried *perished*

[30] fraught *laden*

[34] Yet . . . him *Solanio's reaction to Shylock's grief at losing his daughter with a vessel richly fraught in her possession showed no such tact as this!*

[39] Slubber not business *do not conduct your affair(s) with careless haste*

[40] But . . . time *but give the fullness of time a chance to work for you*

[41] for *as for*

[42] Let . . . love *shut it out of your thoughts – which should be full of love*

[44] ostents *expressions, demonstrations*

[45] As . . . there *as will properly do you credit there*

[46] even there *there and then*

[46–9] *Salerio probably acts out the gestures he is describing, thus balancing a different mood with Solanio's mimicry of Shylock earlier in the scene.*

[48] affection wondrous sensible *remarkably strong emotion*
       sensible *deeply felt on the senses*

[50] I . . . him *I think Antonio's main interest in life is his friendship for Bassanio*

[52] And . . . heaviness *and enliven his cherished melancholy*

I reasoned with a Frenchman yesterday,
Who told me, in the narrow seas that part
The French and English there miscarrièd
A vessel of our country richly fraught.   30
I thought upon Antonio when he told me,
And wished in silence that it were not his.

SOLANIO You were best to tell Antonio what you
        hear –
        Yet do not suddenly, for it may grieve him.

SALERIO A kinder gentleman treads not the earth.
        I saw Bassanio and Antonio part.
        Bassanio told him he would make some speed
        Of his return. He answered, 'Do not so.
        Slubber not business for my sake, Bassanio,
        But stay the very riping of the time;   40
        And for the Jew's bond which he hath of me,
        Let it not enter in your mind of love.
        Be merry, and employ your chiefest thoughts
        To courtship and such fair ostents of love
        As shall conveniently become you there.'
        And even there, his eye being big with tears,
        Turning his face, he put his hand behind him,
        And with affection wondrous sensible
        He wrung Bassanio's hand; and so they parted.

SOLANIO I think he only loves the world for him.   50
        I pray thee let us go and find him out,
        And quicken his embracèd heaviness
        With some delight or other.

SALERIO   Do we so.

                                        [*Exeunt*

ACT TWO, scene 9

[1–3] *This brief little introduction works like a cinema-shot. As the curtains of the inner stage are drawn aside Venice 'fades out' and the main business of the new scene 'fades in'.*

[1] draw the curtain straight   *pull back the curtain straightaway*

[2] Arragon   *A Spanish kingdom. The name also hints at the essence of this suitor's character – an arrogant pride.*

ta'en his oath   *compare II. 1. 44*

[3] to his election presently   *to make his choice immediately*

[9] enjoined   *bound*

[16] injunctions   *conditions*

[18] And so have I addressed me   *and I have sworn so too as a preliminary to viewing the caskets*

Scene 9. *Enter* NERISSA *and a* SERVANT

NERISSA Quick, quick I pray thee, draw the curtain
    straight.
    The Prince of Arragon hath ta'en his oath,
    And comes to his election presently.

Flourish of cornets. Enter the PRINCE OF ARRAGON, *his*
train, and PORTIA

PORTIA Behold, there stand the caskets, noble
    Prince.
    If you choose that wherein I am contained,
    Straight shall our nuptial rites be solemnised;
    But if you fail, without more speech, my lord,
    You must be gone from hence immediately.

ARRAGON I am enjoined by oath to observe three
    things:
    First, never to unfold to anyone   10
    Which casket 'twas I chose; next, if I fail
    Of the right casket, never in my life
    To woo a maid in way of marriage;
    Lastly, if I do fail in fortune of my choice,
    Immediately to leave you and be gone.

PORTIA To these injunctions everyone doth swear
    That comes to hazard for my worthless self.

ARRAGON And so have I addressed me. [*Turning to*
    the caskets] Fortune now
    To my heart's hope! Gold, silver, and base lead.
    'Who chooseth me must give and hazard all he
    hath.'   20
    You shall look fairer ere I give or hazard.
    What says the golden chest? Ha, let me see.
    'Who chooseth me shall gain what many men
    desire.'

[24–9] that 'many' . . . casualty *'that word "many" may mean the stupid mass of the population, people who judge by appearances, accepting what their eyes tell them instead of trying to go to the heart of things; such people base their opinions on surface impressions in the same way as the swift (or the house-martin) builds an exposed nest on the outer wall of a building, just where it may most easily come to harm'. The lines are a beautiful example of pride coming before a fall, or of the biter bit. For it is unwise to base one's judgement on 'show', but Arragon has just done just that in front of the leaden casket (a mistake very apparent to 'the fool multitude' in the audience).*

[26] fond eye *foolish eye*

[31] jump *join in*

[32] barbarous *ignorant and crude. He is an unmitigated snob, the worst kind of aristocrat, full of smug self-satisfaction.*

[34] title *inscription – but there is also some suggestion of the aristocrat's 'title' (the stamp of merit)*

[36–8] for who shall . . . merit *one should not try to cheat one's way out of one's destined lot by aspiring to honour that one is simply unworthy to receive. (In Arragon's view honour and merit can only truly belong to a born nobleman – such as himself!)*

[40–2] O . . . wearer *'If only property, status and official positions were not acquired and handed on in shady ways, so that a pure nobility based on worthiness could be achieved.' Arragon proceeds to hold forth repetitiously on what is obviously his favourite theme.*

[43] cover *put on their hats*

bare *bare-headed. One took off one's hat in the presence of one's social superior.*

[45–8] How . . . varnished *How many low-born folk would then be sifted out from the ranks of the true-born nobility, and how much more resplendent that nobility would appear for being freed from the rubbish that adheres to it these days*

[48] Well, but to my choice *He has been quite carried away on his hobby-horse!*

What many men desire – that 'many' may be
    meant
By the fool multitude that choose by show,
Not learning more than the fond eye doth teach,
Which pries not to th'interior, but like the
    martlet
Builds in the weather on the outward wall,
Even in the force and road of casualty.
I will not choose what many men desire,   30
Because I will not jump with common spirits
And rank me with the barbarous multitudes.
Why then, to thee, thou silver treasure house.
Tell me once more what title thou dost bear.
'Who chooseth me shall get as much as he
    deserves.'
And well said too, for who shall go about
To cozen Fortune, and be honourable
Without the stamp of merit? Let none presume
To wear an undeservèd dignity.
O that estates, degrees, and offices   40
Were not derived corruptly, and that clear
    honour
Were purchased by the merit of the wearer!
How many then should cover that stand bare;
How many be commanded that command;
How much low peasantry would then be
    gleaned
From the true seed of honour; and how much
    honour
Picked from the chaff and ruin of the times
To be new varnished! Well, but to my choice.
'Who chooseth me shall get as much as he
    deserves.'

[50] assume desert   *take it (for granted) that I do indeed deserve to win*

[51] *Possibly this is an order to a servant to carry out the 'menial' task of actually unlocking the casket for Arragon.*

[52] Too long a pause   *Arragon is struck temporarily speechless by what he finds in the casket.*

[53] a blinking idiot   *a fool (or Fool) with a twinkle (or a wink) in his eye*

[54] a schedule   *a scroll*

[55] thou   *the portrait. Arragon has picked up the scroll and the picture together, and dwells on the latter for a moment before reading the former. The plainness of his indignation makes a comic contrast to his recent speechifying.*

[60–61] To offend . . . natures   *Having committed a fault, you cannot expect to weigh it up fairly yourself, since the first action shows that you lack the very power of judgement on which the second depends.*

[63] The fire . . . this   *A reference to the process of refining silver.*

[64–5] Seven . . . amiss   *A flawless power of judgement is as rare, precious, pure and tested as silver is.*

[66] shadows kiss   *embrace illusions instead of reality (as Arragon does with his notion of what 'merit' is, for instance)*

[67] but a shadow's bliss   *only the appearance, not the substance, of happiness*

[68] iwis   *for sure, indeed*

[68–9] There . . . this   *A rich façade can cover a stupid person, just as the silver casket contained the fool's portrait ('this').*

[70] Take . . . bed   *Shakespeare seems to have forgotten for a moment the second condition in Arragon's oath (see ll. 11–13).*

[71] I . . . head   *a fool is what you will always be*

[72] you are sped   *'that's your lot'*

I will assume desert. Give me a key for this,   50
And instantly unlock my fortunes here.

He opens the silver casket

PORTIA [*Aside*] Too long a pause for that which you
    find there.

ARRAGON What's here? The portrait of a blinking
    idiot

Presenting me a schedule! I will read it.
How much unlike art thou to Portia!
How much unlike my hopes and my deserv-
    ings!
'Who chooseth me shall have as much as he
    deserves.'
Did I deserve no more than a fool's head?
Is that my prize? Are my deserts no better?

PORTIA To offend and judge are distinct offices,   60
And of opposèd natures.

ARRAGON [*opening the scroll*] What is here?
    'The fire seven times tried this:
    Seven times tried that judgement is
    That did never choose amiss.
    Some there be that shadows kiss;
    Such have but a shadow's bliss.
    There be fools alive iwis,
    Silvered o'er, and so was this.
    Take what wife you will to bed,   70
    I will ever be your head.
    So be gone; you are sped.'
Still more fool I shall appear
By the time I linger here.
With one fool's head I came to woo,
But I go away with two.

[78] wroth *Possibly for 'ruth' (grief) – but more probably a pretentious man's pretentious word for his indignation at failure.*

[80–1] O . . . lose *Such people go out of their way to make fools of themselves! All their clever-clever reasoning leads them into the wrong choices.*

[82] is no heresy *is quite true*

[83] Compare I. 2. 31–5: *Nerissa is still quite confident that the right choice will be made by the right man for Portia – and Shakespeare promptly brings news of him.*

[84] draw the curtain *The caskets are thus left in place ready for III. 2 on the inner stage.*

[85] What would my lord? *'What does my lord want?' Rid of the threat of Arragon for a husband, Portia jokes with her servant, and the mood of the rest of the scene brightens.*

[89] sensible regreets *greetings both 'strongly felt' and 'substantial' (being accompanied by rich gifts)*

[90] commends and courteous breath *compliments and gracious speech*

[91] Yet *so far*

[92] likely *promising*

[94] costly *bounteous*

[98] Thou . . . him *you seem in such holiday spirits in recommending him*

[100] Quick *lively*
post *messenger*
mannerly *courteously*

[101] Bassanio . . . be *May it be Bassanio, O Cupid!*

[To PORTIA] Sweet, adieu. I'll keep my oath,
Patiently to bear my wroth.

[Exit with his train

PORTIA Thus hath the candle singed the moth.
O these deliberate fools! When they do choose,   80
They have the wisdom by their wit to lose.
NERISSA The ancient saying is no heresy –
'Hanging and wiving goes by destiny.'
PORTIA Come draw the curtain, Nerissa.

Enter MESSENGER

MESSENGER Where is my lady?
PORTIA   Here. What would my lord?
MESSENGER Madam, there is alighted at your gate
A young Venetian, one that comes before
To signify th'approaching of his lord,
From whom he bringeth sensible regreets,
To wit, besides commends and courteous
breath,   90
Gifts of rich value. Yet I have not seen
So likely an ambassador of love.
A day in April never came so sweet
To show how costly summer was at hand,
As this fore-spurrer comes before his lord.
PORTIA No more, I pray thee. I am half afear'd
Thou wilt say anon he is some kin to thee,
Thou spend'st such high-day wit in praising
him.
Come, come, Nerissa, for I long to see
Quick Cupid's post that comes so mannerly.   100
NERISSA Bassanio, Lord Love, if thy will it be!

[Exeunt

ACT THREE, scene 1

As if in response to the 'true love' just heralded in Belmont, this scene brings to the fore true hate – Christian for Jew, Jew for Christian – in Venice. The play will alternate between these two emotional driving forces, each with its attendant hazards, for most of Act Three – with a mounting sense of crisis.

[2] yet it lives there unchecked *still no one denies the report*

[4] the Goodwins *a sandbank ('flat') in the English Channel ('the narrow seas'). Presumably Salerio refers to the same wreck that he mentioned in II. 8. 27–30.*

[7] if my gossip . . . her word *if Old Mother Rumour is telling the truth*

[10] knapped *nibbled. (Ginger sweetened the breath – and hid the smell of drink!)*

[12–13] without any slips . . . highway of talk *to speak plainly and to come straight to the point. (This is just what he is not doing, as Salerio promptly reminds him.)*

[16] Come, the full stop *Get to the end of your sentence*

[21] Let me say 'Amen' . . . cross my prayer *I'll say 'Amen to that at once, in order to seal the prayer before the devil can upset it*

[Enter Shylock] *The passion 'so strange, outrageous, and so variable', that Solanio mocked with such relish in the scene before last, now comes alive upon the stage.*

ACT THREE

Scene 1. *Enter* SOLANIO *and* SALERIO

SOLANIO Now what news on the Rialto?

SALERIO Why, yet it lives there unchecked that
Antonio hath a ship of rich lading wracked on the
narrow seas – the Goodwins I think they call the
place, a very dangerous flat, and fatal, where the
carcasses of many a tall ship lie buried as they
say – if my gossip Report be an honest woman of
her word.

SOLANIO I would she were as lying a gossip in that
as ever knapped ginger or made her neighbours   10
believe she wept for the death of a third husband:
but it is true, without any slips of prolixity or
crossing the plain highway of talk, that the good
Antonio, the honest Antonio – O that I had a
title good enough to keep his name company—

SALERIO Come, the full stop.

SOLANIO Ha, what sayest thou? Why the end is, he
hath lost a ship.

SALERIO I would it might prove the end of his
losses.   20

SOLANIO Let me say 'Amen' betimes lest the devil
cross my prayer, for here he comes in the likeness
of a Jew.

Enter SHYLOCK

How now, Shylock? What news among the
merchants?

SHYLOCK You knew – none so well, none so well as
you – of my daughter's flight.

[31] fledged *feathered and ready to fly*

[31–2] complexion . . . dam *it is the nature of fledgelings to leave their mother*

[34–5] if the devil . . . judge *if the devil himself – and that's you – is sentencing her*

[37–8] Out upon it . . . these years? *By twisting 'flesh and blood' to mean 'sensual desire' Solanio here contrives a cheap dirty joke: 'Shame on you, you rotten old man. Are you feeling sexy at your age?'*

[42] jet *fossil material – very hard, very black*

[44] Rhenish *white wine, reputedly more potent than the common red*

[46] another bad match *As if his daughter had been merely 'a bad bargain', too! The phrase is a revealing one. It brings out the essential and habitual business sense of a man whose flesh-and-blood feelings of human kindness (of belonging to, not just living off, mankind) have been seriously blunted by the way he has been treated. Now it takes extreme force of circumstance to induce him to show such feelings – as he does in his very next speech, with a vengeance.*

[47] a prodigal *compare II. 5. 15 and II. 6. 14–19*

[48–9] so smug *so conscious of his own smartness*

[49] mart *the exchange market, the Rialto*

Let him look to his bond *The repetition is an enacted sneer (at one who is also suffering from an extreme force of circumstance).*

[52] courtesy *kindness (by charging no interest on loans)*

[55] To bait fish withal *To use as bait on a fishing trip (since the flesh cannot serve for human consumption). Compare I. 3. 164–8.*

[56–7] He hath disgraced . . . half a million *He has dishonoured me and kept me from making half a million ducats*

SALERIO That's certain. I (for my part) knew the
tailor that made the wings she flew withal.

SOLANIO And Shylock (for his own part) knew the 30
bird was fledged, and then it is the complexion of
them all to leave the dam.

SHYLOCK She is damned for it.

SALERIO That's certain – if the devil may be her
judge.

SHYLOCK My own flesh and blood to rebel!

SOLANIO Out upon it, old carrion! Rebels it at these
years?

SHYLOCK I say my daughter is my flesh and my
blood. 40

SALERIO There is more difference between thy flesh
and hers than between jet and ivory, more
between your bloods than there is between red
wine and Rhenish. But tell us, do you hear
whether Antonio have had any loss at sea or no?

SHYLOCK There I have another bad match – a bankrupt, a prodigal who dare scarce show his head on
the Rialto, a beggar that was used to come so
smug upon the mart! Let him look to his bond.
He was wont to call me 'usurer'. Let him look to 50
his bond. He was wont to lend money for a
Christian courtesy. Let him look to his bond.

SALERIO Why, I am sure if he forfeit thou wilt not
take his flesh. What's that good for?

SHYLOCK To bait fish withal. If it will feed nothing
else, it will feed my revenge. He hath disgraced me
and hindered me half a million, laughed at my
losses, mocked at my gains, scorned my nation,
thwarted my bargains, cooled my friends, heated
mine enemies – and what's his reason? I am a 60

[62] dimensions *bodily parts*
affections *feelings*

[71] what is his humility? *what is the Christian's humble response?*

[73] sufferance *long-suffering; endurance. Compare I. 3. 111.*

[75–6] it shall go hard ... the. instruction *I shall certainly improve on what I have been taught. (The naked threat, here, shows up the flaw in Shylock's 'argument'. For all the appeal that the heart of his speech makes, and for all his apparent balancing of the issues, the relished 'villainy' of his intended revenge far outweighs the 'villainy' of the wrongs Antonio has done him. Remember 'I hate him for he is a Christian', I. 3. 43. The ancient grudge, more hate-ridden than ever since Jessica's flight with a Christian, does not justify attempted murder, however legally attempted!)*

[79] Tubal *The character may originally have been played by the actor of Old Gobbo. But here Tubal is a serious 'stooge', serving his fellow Jew with information that causes intense woe and savage ecstasy by turns.*

[80–1] A third cannot be matched *One cannot find another Jew as bad as these two*

[87–8] A diamond gone *Again, the loss of his jewels seems more immediately painful to him than the loss of his daughter. Compare II. 8. 12–22.*

Jew. Hath not a Jew eyes? Hath not a Jew hands, organs, dimensions, senses, affections, passions? Fed with the same food, hurt with the same weapons, subject to the same diseases, healed by the same means, warmed and cooled by the same winter and summer as a Christian is? If you prick us, do we not bleed? If you tickle us, do we not laugh? If you poison us, do we not die? And if you wrong us, shall we not revenge? If we are like you in the rest, we will resemble you in that. If a   70 Jew wrong a Christian, what is his humility? Revenge! If a Christian wrong a Jew, what should his sufferance be by Christian example? Why, revenge! The villainy you teach me I will execute, and it shall go hard but I will better the instruction.

Enter a MAN *from* ANTONIO

MAN Gentlemen, my master Antonio is at his house, and desires to speak with you both.

SALERIO We have been up and down to seek him.

Enter TUBAL

SOLANIO Here comes another of the tribe. A third   80 cannot be matched, unless the devil himself turn Jew.

               [*Exeunt* SOLANIO, SALERIO *and* MAN

SHYLOCK How now, Tubal? What news from Genoa? Hast thou found my daughter?

TUBAL I often came where I did hear of her, but cannot find her.

SHYLOCK Why there, there, there, there! A diamond gone cost me two thousand ducats in Frankfort –

[93] hearsed   *in her coffin*

[99] but what lights o'   *except what alights upon*

[117] divers of   *a number of*
[119] break   *go bankrupt*

the curse never fell upon our nation till now; I
never felt it till now – two thousand ducats in   90
that, and other precious, precious jewels. I would
my daughter were dead at my foot, and the jewels
in her ear! Would she were hearsed at my foot,
and the ducats in her coffin! No news of them?
Why, so! And I know not what's spent in the
search. Why thou loss upon loss – the thief gone
with so much, and so much to find the thief –
and no satisfaction, no revenge, nor no ill luck
stirring but what lights o'my shoulders, no sighs
but o'my breathing, no tears but o'my shedding.   100

TUBAL Yes, other men have ill luck too. Antonio,
as I heard in Genoa—

SHYLOCK What, what, what? Ill luck, ill luck?

TUBAL —hath an argosy cast away coming from
Tripolis.

SHYLOCK I thank God, I thank God! Is it true, is it
true?

TUBAL I spoke with some of the sailors that escaped
the wrack.

SHYLOCK I thank thee, good Tubal. Good news,   110
good news! Ha, ha! Heard in Genoa?

TUBAL Your daughter spent in Genoa, as I heard,
one night, fourscore ducats.

SHYLOCK Thou stick'st a dagger in me. I shall never
see my gold again. Fourscore ducats at a sitting,
fourscore ducats!

TUBAL There came divers of Antonio's creditors in
my company to Venice that swear he cannot
choose but break.

SHYLOCK I am very glad of it. I'll plague him; I'll   120
torture him. I am glad of it.

[125] **Leah** *Shylock's wife (now, presumably, dead)*

[130] **fee me an officer** *pay for an officer-of-the-law (to arrest Antonio)*

bespeak him *engage his services*

[131] **I will have . . . forfeit** *Shylock means this literally. No doubt he had the words 'nearest his heart' inserted when the notary actually wrote out the bond. See I. 3. 151–2 and IV. 1. 253.*

[132–3] **make what merchandise I will** *do as much business as I like*

ACT THREE, scene 2

The play's third, and main, casket scene opens quite differently from the two earlier ones: no fanfares, no speechifying from self-important suitors – just a quiet, drawn-out, embarrassed avowal of her feelings from Portia in tête-à-tête conversation with Bassanio (in marked contrast to the fierce accents of hatred just heard in Venice). For the first thirty-nine lines of the scene Portia probably keeps Bassanio downstage, near to the audience but away from 'all their trains' (including the musicians, who may be stationed in the gallery above the inner stage). The caskets stand in readiness – see II. 9. 84.

[4] **(but it is not love)** *The nervous, hesitant expression indicates how strongly she* does *feel for him!*

[5] **I would not** *I have no wish to*

[6] **Hate . . . quality** *this kind of declaration (that is, 'I would not lose you') does not arise from hostile feelings*

[8] **And yet . . . thought** *but a girl can only say what she thinks*

[11] **I am forsworn** *I would have broken my promise (to my father)*

[14–15] **Beshrew your eyes . . . divided me!** *Shame on you for looking at me so bewitchingly and setting me at odds with myself!*

TUBAL One of them showed me a ring that he had
of your daughter for a monkey.

SHYLOCK Out upon her! Thou torturest me, Tubal.
It was my turquoise; I had it of Leah when I was
a bachelor. I would not have given it for a
wilderness of monkeys.

TUBAL But Antonio is certainly undone.

SHYLOCK Nay, that's true, that's very true. Go,
Tubal, fee me an officer; bespeak him a fortnight 130
before. I will have the heart of him if he forfeit,
for were he out of Venice I can make what merchandise I will. Go, Tubal, and meet me at our
synagogue; go, good Tubal; at our synagogue,
Tubal.

[*Exeunt*

Scene 2. *Enter* BASSANIO, PORTIA, GRATIANO, NERISSA,
and all their trains

PORTIA I pray you tarry; pause a day or two
Before you hazard, for in choosing wrong
I lose your company. Therefore forbear awhile.
There's something tells me (but it is not love)
I would not lose you; and you know yourself
Hate counsels not in such a quality.
But lest you should not understand me well –
And yet a maiden hath no tongue but thought –
I would detain you here some month or two
Before you venture for me. I could teach you   10
How to choose right, but then I am forsworn.
So will I never be. So may you miss me.
But if you do, you'll make me wish a sin –
That I had been forsworn. Beshrew your eyes,
They have o'erlooked me and divided me!

THE MERCHANT OF VENICE

[17] I would *I feel I ought to*

[18–19] O these naughty times . . . rights! *'In these wicked days one is prevented from possessing what rightfully belongs to one!' She thinks of Bassanio as 'owner' and of herself as the thing owned.*

[20] Prove it so *if it should so turn out (that I cannot belong to you as your wife)*

[21] Let Fortune . . . not I *may Fortune be damned for it, for it will be her fault, not mine (as I will not commit the sin of forswearing)*

[22] piece *fill out (as, for instance, a tailor might enlarge a garment by stitching into it an extra piece of material)*

[23] eke *add to*

[24] stay you from election *keep you from choosing*

[25] I live upon the rack *Until he has gone through the casket test, Bassanio is tortured by uncertainty about his future state. He picks up the image of the rack from Portia's reference to drawing time 'out in length' (l. 23).*

[26–7] Then confess . . . your love *She (playfully) gives Bassanio's expression an unexpected twist here. The rack was the standard torture-instrument for extorting confessions from traitors.*

[29] fear th'enjoying of my love *afraid that I may not win you as my wife*

[30] There may as well be amity *it is as easy for there to be friendliness*

[33] enforcèd *who are forced (by torture)*

[35] confess and live *(instead of being tortured to death for keeping the truth secret)*

[35–6] 'Confess' . . . confession! *Two words – 'confess love' – would sum up the whole truth of what I would have to say to you!*

[38] for deliverance *resulting in my release*

[39] let me to *let me go to*

[40] Away then! *She breaks off their tête-à-tête, knowing, as Bassanio does, that real 'deliverance' from the tension they both feel will come only after the casket test has been faced. It may be at this moment that the inner stage curtains are drawn back to reveal the caskets.*

[42] all aloof *well out of the way. Portia is both mistress of the house and 'stage-manager' of the scene at this point. As the onlookers draw back, Bassanio moves upstage towards the caskets. No doubt he makes some preparation on the way (such as a ceremonial oath-taking?) since it seems that he does not actually reach the caskets for another twenty lines.*

[44] swanlike end *It was part of Elizabethan lore that the swan, a mute bird, would sing, once only, sweetly and sorrowfully, just before its death.*

One half of me is yours, the other half yours –
'Mine own' I would say; but if mine, then
    yours;
And so all yours. O these naughty times
Put bars between the owners and their rights!
And so, though yours, not yours. Prove it so,   20
Let Fortune go to hell for it, not I.
I speak too long, but 'tis to piece the time,
To eke it and to draw it out in length,
To stay you from election.

BASSANIO   Let me choose,
For as I am, I live upon the rack.

PORTIA Upon the rack, Bassanio? Then confess
What treason there is mingled with your love.

BASSANIO None but that ugly treason of mistrust
Which makes me fear th'enjoying of my love.
There may as well be amity and life   30
'Tween snow and fire, as treason and my love.

PORTIA Ay, but I fear you speak upon the rack,
Where men enforcèd do speak anything.

BASSANIO Promise me life, and I'll confess the truth.

PORTIA Well then, confess and live.

BASSANIO   'Confess' and 'love'
Had been the very sum of my confession!
O happy torment, when my torturer
Doth teach me answers for deliverance.
But let me to my fortune and the caskets.

PORTIA Away then! I am locked in one of them;   40
If you do love me, you will find me out.
Nerissa and the rest, stand all aloof.
Let music sound while he doth make his
    choice;
Then if he lose he makes a swanlike end,

THE MERCHANT OF VENICE

[46] stand more proper   *fit even more exactly*
    my eye shall be the stream   *I will weep copiously (if you choose wrongly). (A passage of semi-soliloquy, spoken half to herself and half to the onlookers, begins here.)*

[49] flourish   *fanfare*

[50–5] Such it is . . . to marriage   *It was the custom to play music to waken a bridegroom on the morning of his wedding day.*

[51] dulcet   *sweet*

[53] Now he goes   *Bassanio draws nearer to the caskets.*

[53–7] Now he goes . . . sea monster   *Hercules (otherwise known as Alcides) saved a Trojan princess, Hesione, from being sacrificed to a sea-monster (which he killed). He did this to win a reward of some fine horses, offered by her father, not out of love for the lady.*

[57] I stand for sacrifice   *I am like that princess*

[58] The rest aloof   *see [42]*
    Dardanian wives   *Trojan women*

[59] blearèd visages   *tear-stained faces*

[60] issue   *outcome*

[61] Live thou   *if you live*
    dismay   *alarm and distress*

[Music. A song]   *The music may well have begun at l. 43 as an introduction to the song that now follows. Its words and melody, like the gracious and heroic imagery in Portia's speech, help to refine and dignify the loving atmosphere, giving the occasion an intensity that the previous casket scenes lack.*

[63] Fancy   *light-hearted love of pleasure*

[64] Or . . . or   *Is it . . . or is it*

[67–9] It is engendered . . . it lies   *Most appropriately to the occasion, the song warns that Fancy, unlike true Love, is bred on what merely pleases the eye, and so its life-span is very brief.*

[70] knell   *funeral bell*

Fading in music. That the comparison
May stand more proper, my eye shall be the
   stream
And watery death-bed for him. He may win,
And what is music then? Then music is
Even as the flourish when true subjects bow
To a new-crownèd monarch. Such it is   50
As are those dulcet sounds in break of day
That creep into the dreaming bridegroom's ear
And summon him to marriage. Now he goes,
With no less presence but with much more love
Than young Alcides when he did redeem
The virgin tribute paid by howling Troy
To the sea monster. I stand for sacrifice;
The rest aloof are the Dardanian wives,
With blearèd visages come forth to view
The issue of the exploit. Go, Hercules!   60
Live thou, I live. With much, much more dis-
   may
I view the fight, than thou that mak'st the fray.

Music. A song while BASSANIO *comments on the caskets to
himself*

      Tell me where is Fancy bred –
      Or in the heart, or in the head?
      How begot, how nourishèd?
        Reply, reply.
      It is engendered in the eyes,
      With gazing fed, and Fancy dies
      In the cradle where it lies.
        Let us all ring Fancy's knell.   70
        I'll begin it – ding, dong, bell.
ALL   Ding, dong, bell.

THE MERCHANT OF VENICE

[73] So . . . *The song's 'message' is certainly not lost on Bassanio.*

be least themselves *give no sign of what things are really like*

[74] The world . . . ornament *people everywhere are led astray by false appearances*

[75–7] In law . . . evil? *A lawyer can often disguise a rotten cause, condoning wickedness with his smooth tongue. (The analogy is with stale meat which has to be heavily spiced – 'seasoned' – to cover the bad taste.)*

[79] approve *uphold*

a text *a quotation from the Bible*

[81] simple *plain, unadulterated*

[82] his *its*

[83–4] false . . . sand *Steps cut in sand-hills are notoriously liable to let you down suddenly.*

[85] Hercules . . . Mars *Legendary strong man and god of war. They represent an ideal courage.*

[86] livers white as milk *The liver was supposed to be the bodily source of courage. Cowards' livers were thought to be pale because bloodless.*

[87–8] And these . . . redoubted *Such cowards merely adopt the bearded appearance of bravery to make themselves seem formidable.*

[88] beauty *He has in mind beauty of the applied, cosmetic sort.*

[91] lightest *A pun on the two senses 'lightweight' and 'light in virtue' (like a painted whore).*

[92] crispèd *curly*

[93] make such wanton gambols *play so mischievously*

[94] Upon supposèd fairness *on the head of a so-called beauty*

[95] dowry *endowment (wigs were often made from the hair of corpses)*

[97] guilèd *guileful, treacherously attractive*

[99] an Indian beauty *a dark-skinned 'beauty'. (To the Elizabethans a fair skin, like Portia's, was essential to true beauty.)*

BASSANIO So may the outward shows be least them-
        selves;
    The world is still deceived with ornament.
    In law, what plea so tainted and corrupt,
    But being seasoned with a gracious voice,
    Obscures the show of evil? In religion,
    What damnèd error but some sober brow
    Will bless it and approve it with a text,
    Hiding the grossness with fair ornament?   80
    There is no vice so simple but assumes
    Some mark of virtue on his outward parts.
    How many cowards, whose hearts are all as
        false
    As stairs of sand, wear yet upon their chins
    The beards of Hercules and frowning Mars,
    Who inward searched have livers white as milk?
    And these assume but valour's excrement
    To render them redoubted. Look on beauty,
    And you shall see 'tis purchased by the weight,
    Which therein works a miracle in nature,   90
    Making them lightest that wear most of it.
    So are those crispèd snaky golden locks,
    Which make such wanton gambols with the
        wind
    Upon supposèd fairness, often known
    To be the dowry of a second head,
    The skull that bred them in the sepulchre.
    Thus ornament is but the guilèd shore
    To a most dangerous sea, the beauteous scarf
    Veiling an Indian beauty; in a word,
    The seeming truth which cunning times put on 100
    To entrap the wisest. Therefore thou gaudy
        gold,

[102] Hard food for Midas   *In Greek legend greedy King Midas was granted his wish that everything he touched should turn to gold. He had a lot of trouble at meal-times.*

[103] pale and common drudge   *Much of the coinage by which everyday business was carried on was made of silver, a pale metal (in comparison with gold).*

[104] meagre   *bare and unattractive*

[105] Which rather threaten'st   *The 'threat' lies in the casket's plain, blunt inscription.*

[107] Joy be the consequence!   *And Portia's joy is the immediate consequence, breaking out in the lilt of rhymed couplets.*

[108] fleet to air   *vanish away*

[109] As   *such as*

[112] In measure . . . excess   *Keep this overflowing happiness controlled within reasonable limits!*

[114] surfeit   *fall ill through having too much*

[115] counterfeit   *portrait*

demi-god   *a maker who must have been half-divine (to have painted such a lifelike image)*

[115–26] *Bassanio's praise of Portia's picture here blends the extravagant rapture of the moment (he has just hazarded 'all he hath' – and won!) with good manners. Extravagant compliments to his lady were expected from a courtly lover (compare, for instance, II. 7. 38–48) and all the more so from a successful one.*

[117] whether   *is it rather that*

the balls of mine   *my eyeballs*

[118] severed   *slightly opened*

[120] sunder   *separate*

[125–6] to steal . . . unfurnished   *to blind him with its beauty, so disabling him from painting her second eye*

unfurnished   *unprovided with a companion*

Hard food for Midas, I will none of thee;
Nor none of thee, thou pale and common
    drudge
'Tween man and man. But thou, thou meagre
    lead
Which rather threaten'st than dost promise
    aught,
Thy paleness moves me more than eloquence,
And here choose I. Joy be the consequence!

PORTIA [*Aside*] How all the other passions fleet to
    air,
As doubtful thoughts, and rash-embraced des-
    pair,
And shudd'ring fear, and green-eyed jealousy. 110
O Love, be moderate, allay thy ecstasy,
In measure rain thy joy, scant this excess!
I fear too much thy blessing; make it less
For fear I surfeit.

BASSANIO [*Opening the leaden casket*]
                What find I here?
Fair Portia's counterfeit! What demi-god
Hath come so near creation? Move these eyes?
Or whether, riding on the balls of mine,
Seem they in motion? Here are severed lips
Parted with sugar breath; so sweet a bar
Should sunder such sweet friends. Here in her
    hairs   120
The painter plays the spider, and hath woven
A golden mesh t'entrap the hearts of men
Faster than gnats in cobwebs. But her eyes –
How could he see to do them? Having made one,
Methinks it should have power to steal both his
And leave itself unfurnished. Yet look how far

[127] substance of my praise   *all that my praise amounts to*
[127, 128] this shadow   *this picture*

[129] the substance   *the original, Portia herself*

[130] continent   *container*

[132] Chance . . . true   *May your fortune be as fair and your judgement as true (as Portia is)*

[140] by note   *as instructed (by the scroll)*

[141] contending in a prize   *competing against each other*
[141-6]   *Perhaps this comparison occurs to Bassanio as a consequence of the warm reception his 'claiming' of Portia receives from the spectators on the stage.*

[145] his   *for him*

[148] ratified   *validated*
[148, 150-60, 167-72]   *As Portia and Bassanio formally 'bind' their love to each other, they borrow terms of legal practice, banking, property-owning – Venice terms. And other 'bondage', from Venice, will soon actually appear to disturb the Belmont scene (ll. 219-20).*

The substance of my praise doth wrong this
   shadow
In underprizing it; so far this shadow
Doth limp behind the substance. Here's the
   scroll,
The continent and summary of my fortune.   130
   'You that choose not by the view
   Chance as fair, and choose as true.
   Since this fortune falls to you,
   Be content and seek no new.
   If you be well pleased with this
   And hold your fortune for your bliss,
   Turn you where your lady is
   And claim her with a loving kiss.'
A gentle scroll. Fair lady, by your leave,
I come by note, to give and to receive.   140

He kisses her

Like one of two contending in a prize
That thinks he hath done well in people's eyes,
Hearing applause and universal shout,
Giddy in spirit, still gazing in a doubt
Whether those peals of praise be his or no,
So, thrice-fair lady, stand I, even so –
As doubtful whether what I see be true,
Until confirmed, signed, ratified by you.
PORTIA You see me, Lord Bassanio, where I stand,
   Such as I am. Though for myself alone   150
I would not be ambitious in my wish
To wish myself much better, yet for you
I would be trebled twenty times myself,
A thousand times more fair, ten thousand times
More rich—

[156] account *opinion*

[157] livings *possessions*

[158] Exceed account *go beyond all reckoning*

[158–60] But . . . unpractised *But all that I am amounts to nothing – that is, all in all, a girl with no learning, no training, no experience in the ways of the world*

[164–6] Happiest . . . king *As the rest of the play will show, this model of wifely submission is Portia's ideal self rather than her real one!*

[167–8] to you . . . converted *now belongs to you*

[168] But now *just now*

[170] even now, but now *at this very moment*

[172] I give them with this ring *In this way Portia gives Bassanio the 'ratification' that he asked for (148). Like a wedding ring, this ring is symbolically the assurance* and the requirement *of loyalty in love, both spiritual and physical. It represents a bond of body and soul – which is the serious point underlying the comedy about it in Acts Four and Five.*

[174] presage *predict*

[175] be my . . . on you *justify my speaking out against you*

[178] powers *(of speech and thought)*

[182–3] Where . . . joy *when each particular response, mixed with all the others, contributes to a general blur of noise that has no precise form but conveys the public happiness nonetheless*

That only to stand high in your account,
I might in virtues, beauties, livings, friends,
Exceed account. But the full sum of me
Is sum of nothing – which, to term in gross,
Is an unlessoned girl, unschooled, unpractised; 160
Happy in this, she is not yet so old
But she may learn; happier than this,
She is not bred so dull but she can learn;
Happiest of all is that her gentle spirit
Commits itself to yours to be directed,
As from her lord, her governor, her king.
Myself, and what is mine, to you and yours
Is now converted. But now I was the lord
Of this fair mansion, master of my servants,
Queen o'er myself; and even now, but now, 170
This house, these servants, and this same my-
    self
Are yours, my lord's. I give them with this
    ring,
Which when you part from, lose, or give
    away,
Let it presage the ruin of your love
And be my vantage to exclaim on you.
BASSANIO Madam, you have bereft me of all words.
Only my blood speaks to you in my veins,
And there is such confusion in my powers
As, after some oration fairly spoke
By a belovèd Prince, there doth appear   180
Among the buzzing pleasèd multitude,
Where every something being blent together
Turns to a wild of nothing, save of joy
Expressed and not expressed. But when this
    ring

[191] that you can wish   *that you can desire for yourselves*

[192] you can wish none from me   *you won't wish to deprive me of any of my own joy*

[194] The bargain of your faith   *your loving contract*

[196] so   *provided that*

[200] intermission   *shilly-shallying, time-wasting*

[204] until I sweat again   *so hard that I was repeatedly in a sweat with the effort*

[205] my very roof   *even the roof of my mouth*

[206] (if promise last)   *(if promises can be trusted to last)*

[200–209] *Gratiano's surprising love-affair (a sort of down-to-earth parody of Bassanio's progress at Belmont) acts as a dramatic safety-valve, releasing some of the intensity accumulated from the casket test and lightening the scene before the dark news from Venice is announced.*

[210] so   *so long as*

[211] mean good faith   *both 'speak sincerely' and 'intend to be true'*

[212] faith   *'indeed I do'. True Love, be it noted, is not reserved exclusively for rich and genteel folk!*

Parts from this finger, then parts life from
    hence.
O then be bold to say Bassanio's dead!
NERISSA My lord and lady, it is now our time
    That have stood by and seen our wishes
    prosper,
    To cry 'good joy'. Good joy, my lord and lady!
GRATIANO My Lord Bassanio, and my gentle lady, 190
    I wish you all the joy that you can wish –
    For I am sure you can wish none from me –
    And when your honours mean to solemnise
    The bargain of your faith, I do beseech you
    Even at that time I may be married too.
BASSANIO With all my heart, so thou canst get a
    wife.
GRATIANO I thank your lordship, you have got me
    one.
    My eyes, my lord, can look as swift as yours:
    You saw the mistress, I beheld the maid.
    You loved, I loved – for intermission   200
    No more pertains to me, my lord, than you.
    Your fortune stood upon the caskets there,
    And so did mine too, as the matter falls;
    For wooing here until I sweat again,
    And swearing till my very roof was dry
    With oaths of love, at last (if promise last)
    I got a promise of this fair one here
    To have her love, provided that your fortune
    Achieved her mistress.
PORTIA   Is this true, Nerissa?
NERISSA Madam, it is, so you stand pleasèd withal. 210
BASSANIO And do you, Gratiano, mean good faith?
GRATIANO Yes, faith, my lord.

[214] We'll . . . ducats *We'll bet them a thousand ducats that our son and heir will be born before theirs.*

[216] What . . . down? *And put our money on the table to back up the bet?*

[217, 218] No . . . down *No, it's a hopeless idea if we have to show our money before the game starts. (But Gratiano is also making a blue joke of the phrase 'stake down'.)*

[211–18] *It may not be by accident that Shakespeare heralds the arrival of Lorenzo and Jessica at Belmont with lines that dwell on 'good faith', 'play' and 'ducats'!*

[219] infidel *both 'non-Christian' and 'unfaithful one'. Gratiano uses the word light-heartedly. Since Jessica has become a Christian by marriage, it is no longer accurate, in its first sense at least.*

[222–3] If that . . . power *if my having become lord of Belmont in the last few minutes gives me the right*

[224] very *true. Strangely, he welcomes 'friends and countrymen', but not Jessica (ungreeted until l. 238). Perhaps she is left thus in the background lest the elopement should draw too much of the audience's interest from the news in Antonio's letter to Bassanio.*

[230] past all saying nay *and would not take 'no' for an answer*

[232] reason for it *Presumably Salerio thinks that Lorenzo and Jessica will be able to help (with money? with advice?) in the crisis that he is about to reveal.*

[233] Commends him to you *sends you his kindest regards*
      Ere *before*

[235] Not sick . . . mind *Knowing how bad the news is, Salerio makes a deliberately evasive reply – Antonio is not ill, but he is depressed . . .*

BASSANIO Our feast shall be much honoured in your
    marriage.

GRATIANO [*To* NERISSA] We'll play with them the
    first boy for a thousand ducats.

NERISSA What, and stake down?

GRATIANO No, we shall ne'er win at that sport, and
    stake down.

    But who comes here? Lorenzo and his infidel!

    What, and my old Venetian friend Salerio!   220

Enter LORENZO, JESSICA *and* SALERIO (*a messenger from*
Venice)

BASSANIO Lorenzo and Salerio, welcome hither,
    If that the youth of my new interest here
    Have power to bid you welcome. [*To* PORTIA]
      By your leave,
    I bid my very friends and countrymen,
    Sweet Portia, welcome.

PORTIA   So do I, my lord.
    They are entirely welcome.

LORENZO I thank your honour. For my part, my lord,
    My purpose was not to have seen you here,
    But meeting with Salerio by the way,
    He did entreat me past all saying nay   230
    To come with him along.

SALERIO   I did, my lord,
    And I have reason for it. Signior Antonio
    Commends him to you.

He gives BASSANIO *a letter*

BASSANIO   Ere I ope his letter,
    I pray you tell me how my good friend doth.

SALERIO Not sick, my lord, unless it be in mind,

[236] Nor well . . . mind . . . *and nothing is well with him, except the fortitude of his spirit.*

[237] estate *condition*

[238] cheer yond stranger *Nerissa joins Jessica and Lorenzo on one side of the stage* . . .

[239] Your hand, Salerio . . . *and Gratiano draws Salerio to the (other?) side, leaving Bassanio to read the letter at the centre of things, with Portia nearby, looking on.*

[240–2] *Antonio's past business successes have made him 'king' of all the merchants in Venice, but here in Belmont Bassanio and Gratiano have met with a success that is equally 'golden' (compare I. 1. 170–3).*

[242] fleece *Perhaps a pun on 'fleets' is intended. In any case, Salerio takes the wind out of Gratiano's sails.*

[244] shrewd contents *hurtful news*

[247] turn so much the constitution *cause such a change in the composure*

[248] constant *steady, well-balanced*

[249] With leave *let me say this*

[255–6] all the wealth . . . my veins *though I had no personal fortune I was of gentle birth*

[258] Rating *in assessing*

[259] How much I was a braggart *how conceited and boastful I was*

Nor well, unless in mind. His letter there
Will show you his estate.

BASSANIO *opens the letter*

GRATIANO Nerissa, cheer yond stranger; bid her
welcome.
Your hand, Salerio. What's the news from
Venice?
How doth that royal merchant, good Antonio? 240
I know he will be glad of our success—
We are the Jasons, we have won the fleece.
SALERIO I would you had won the fleece that he hath
lost.
PORTIA [*Aside*] There are some shrewd contents in
yond same paper
That steals the colour from Bassanio's cheek:
Some dear friend dead, else nothing in the
world
Could turn so much the constitution
Of any constant man. What, worse and worse?
[*Going up to him*] With leave, Bassanio, I am
half yourself,
And I must freely have the half of anything 250
That this same paper brings you.
BASSANIO   O sweet Portia,
Here are a few of the unpleasant'st words
That ever blotted paper! Gentle lady,
When I did first impart my love to you,
I freely told you all the wealth I had
Ran in my veins. I was a gentleman,
And then I told you true; and yet, dear lady,
Rating myself at nothing, you shall see
How much I was a braggart. When I told you

THE MERCHANT OF VENICE

[260] state *fortune*

[262] engaged *bound*
[263] mere *absolute*
[264] To feed my means *in order to get the money I needed*

[268] hit *hit the mark (by reaching its destination safely)*

[270] Barbary *Northwest Africa*

[272] merchant-marring rocks *rocks which destroy merchant* ships

[274] present *ready*
      discharge *repay*
[275] He *Shylock*
[277] keen and greedy *savagely eager (like a ravenous beast)*
      confound *destroy*
[278] plies *urges his case on*
[279] impeach the freedom of the state *threatens to bring the charge that Venice is not observing the principles of non-discrimination on which it was founded as a 'free' city*
[281–2] magnificoes . . . port *the most stately noblemen in Venice's ruling class*
[282] persuaded *pleaded*
[283] envious plea *malicious claim*

My state was nothing, I should then have told
   you   260
That I was worse than nothing; for indeed
I have engaged myself to a dear friend,
Engaged my friend to his mere enemy
To feed my means. Here is a letter, lady,
The paper as the body of my friend,
And every word in it a gaping wound
Issuing life-blood. But is it true, Salerio?
Hath all his ventures failed? What, not one hit?
From Tripolis, from Mexico and England,
From Lisbon, Barbary, and India,   270
And not one vessel scape the dreadful touch
Of merchant-marring rocks?

SALERIO   Not one, my lord.
Besides, it should appear that if he had
The present money to discharge the Jew,
He would not take it. Never did I know
A creature that did bear the shape of man
So keen and greedy to confound a man.
He plies the Duke at morning and at night,
And doth impeach the freedom of the state
If they deny him justice. Twenty merchants, 280
The Duke himself, and the magnificoes
Of greatest port have all persuaded with him,
But none can drive him from the envious plea
Of forfeiture, of justice, and his bond.

JESSICA When I was with him, I have heard him
   swear
To Tubal and to Chus, his countrymen,
That he would rather have Antonio's flesh
Than twenty times the value of the sum
That he did owe him: and I know, my lord,

[293–7] *In these five lines Shakespeare balances Antonio's essential kindness against Shylock's essential malice (283–7).*

[294–5] The best-conditioned . . . courtesies *a man with a most willing and tireless disposition for helping others*

[296] ancient Roman honour *an unwavering loyalty to one's friends and to one's standards of right and wrong (a quality for which many Romans in the course of history – notably Brutus, see I. 1. 167 – have been famous)*

[300] deface *cancel (by destroying)*

[300–5] Pay him . . . friend *Portia's generosity is as extensive as her fortune (not least in acknowledging that 'a friend of this description' has first claim on her husband, in these circumstances) but she has not yet had time to reflect on what Jessica has just said (285–9). By scene 4, though, she has.*

[303] through Bassanio's fault *on Bassanio's account*

[312] shall hence *must leave here*

[313] show a merry cheer *look happy*

[314] dear bought *expensively 'purchased' as a husband (through this plan)*

dear *heartily (and that is a good reason to 'show a merry cheer')*

  If law, authority, and power deny not,   290
  It will go hard with poor Antonio.

PORTIA Is it your dear friend that is thus in trouble?

BASSANIO The dearest friend to me, the kindest man,
  The best-conditioned and unwearied spirit
  In doing courtesies, and one in whom
  The ancient Roman honour more appears
  Than any that draws breath in Italy.

PORTIA What sum owes he the Jew?

BASSANIO For me, three thousand ducats.

PORTIA   What, no more?
  Pay him six thousand, and deface the bond. 300
  Double six thousand, and then treble that,
  Before a friend of this description
  Shall lose a hair through Bassanio's fault.
  First go with me to church and call me wife,
  And then away to Venice to your friend;
  For never shall you lie by Portia's side
  With an unquiet soul. You shall have gold
  To pay the petty debt twenty times over.
  When it is paid, bring your true friend along.
  My maid Nerissa and myself meantime 310
  Will live as maids and widows. Come away,
  For you shall hence upon your wedding day.
  Bid your friends welcome, show a merry cheer;
  Since you are dear bought, I will love you dear.
  But let me hear the letter of your friend.

BASSANIO [*Reads*] *Sweet Bassanio, my ships have all miscarried, my creditors grow cruel, my estate is very low, my bond to the Jew is forfeit. And since in paying it, it is impossible I should live, all debts are cleared between you and I if I might but see you at* 320

[321] Notwithstanding ... pleasure   *however, do as you please*

[323] *Portia's reply is an act of punning on 322. She, as Bassanio's 'love', immediately, does 'persuade him to come' to Antonio.*

[325–8] Since ... twain   *The rhyming quatrain lends a touch of tenderness to the abrupt close of the scene.*

ACT THREE, scene 3

There is no pause between the scenes. As the Belmont characters hurry off at one side of the stage, the Venetians appear from the other. It is as though Shylock and Antonio (who is now under arrest, and probably chained) step alive out of the 'pictures' of themselves in the last fifty lines.

[1] look to him   *keep close guard over him. (The next line-and-a-half is probably spoken to Solanio, who has been trying to plead for his friend.)*
[2] gratis   *interest-free*
[5] I have sworn an oath   *compare I. 3. 47–53 and IV. 1. 227–8.*

[9] naughty   *good-for-nothing*
    fond   *soft-hearted, and therefore foolish*
[10] abroad   *out-of-doors*

[14] dull-eyed   *gullible*

*my death. Notwithstanding, use your pleasure – if
your love do not persuade you to come, let not my
letter.*

PORTIA O love, dispatch all business and be gone!

BASSANIO Since I have your good leave to go away,
    I will make haste, but till I come again
No bed shall e'er be guilty of my stay,
    Nor rest be interposer 'twixt us twain.

[Exeunt

Scene 3. *Enter* SHYLOCK *the Jew,* SOLANIO, ANTONIO *and
the* GAOLER

SHYLOCK Gaoler, look to him. Tell not me of mercy.
    This is the fool that lent out money gratis.
    Gaoler, look to him.

ANTONIO   Hear me yet, good Shylock.

SHYLOCK I'll have my bond – speak not against my
    bond!
    I have sworn an oath that I will have my bond.
    Thou call'dst me 'dog' before thou hadst a
    cause,
    But since I am a dog, beware my fangs.
    The Duke shall grant me justice. I do wonder,
    Thou naughty gaoler, that thou art so fond
    To come abroad with him at his request.   10

ANTONIO I pray thee hear me speak.

SHYLOCK I'll have my bond. I will not hear thee
    speak.
    I'll have my bond, and therefore speak no more.
    I'll not be made a soft and dull-eyed fool,
    To shake the head, relent, and sigh, and yield

[16] intercessors   *pleaders*

[17]   *In this brief appearance, all the main features of Shylock's attacking tactics in the trial scene have been prefigured. Here, as there, they are punctuated and upheld by his gloating reliance on the bond.*

[18] impenetrable   *hard-hearted*

[19] kept   *lived*

[20] bootless   *useless*

[22] delivered from his forfeitures   *released from his clutches (by paying their outstanding debts)*

[25] Will never . . . hold   *will never agree that the penalty in the bond should stand*

[26] deny   *block, over-rule*

[27–31] For . . . nations   *'If the right of aliens to live and work freely here is squashed in this case, then Venetian justice itself will be under suspicion (and this will do much harm) since the city's commercial prosperity depends on international dealings.' This is very much a respectable businessman's way of thinking. Antonio really lives up to the title 'the Merchant of Venice' at this point.*

[32] so bated me   *caused me to lose so much weight*

ACT THREE, scene 4

The momentum of the play continues uninterrupted. The last two lines spoken in Venice lead into the opening theme here – the bond of friendship.

[2] conceit   *conception, understanding*

[3] amity   *friendship ('god-like' because it can inspire devotion as strong as that roused by the goddess of love)*

[4] the absence of your lord   *Bassanio has left for Venice with Gratiano, immediately after the weddings (as decided at III. 2. 324–8).*

To Christian intercessors. Follow not.
I'll have no speaking – I will have my bond.

[*Exit*

SOLANIO It is the most impenetrable cur
That ever kept with men.

ANTONIO   Let him alone.
I'll follow him no more with bootless prayers. 20
He seeks my life. His reason well I know:
I oft delivered from his forfeitures
Many that have at times made moan to me.
Therefore he hates me.

SOLANIO   I am sure the Duke
Will never grant this forfeiture to hold.

ANTONIO The Duke cannot deny the course of law:
For the commodity that strangers have
With us in Venice, if it be denied,
Will much impeach the justice of the state,
Since that the trade and profit of the city   30
Consisteth of all nations. Therefore go.
These griefs and losses have so bated me
That I shall hardly spare a pound of flesh
Tomorrow to my bloody creditor.
Well, gaoler, on. Pray God Bassanio come
To see me pay his debt, and then I care not.

[*Exeunt*

Scene 4. *Enter* PORTIA, NERISSA, LORENZO, JESSICA *and*
BALTHASAR, *a man of Portia's*

LORENZO Madam, although I speak it in your
            presence,
You have a noble and a true conceit
Of god-like amity, which appears most strongly
In bearing thus the absence of your lord.

155

[5] to whom you show this honour   *that is, Antonio*

[7] How dear a lover   *compare III. 2. 292–3 and 321–3*

[8–9] prouder . . . enforce you   *even prouder of this act than you would be of one of your everyday kindnesses*

[12] waste   *spend (the sense of wastefulness is not implied)*

[13–15] Whose souls . . . of lineaments   *(in friends) who are equally strongly attached to each other, there is bound to be a matching balance of characteristics*

[17] the bosom lover   *the intimate friend*

[18] Must needs be like my lord   *This idea – that partners in a love-relationship resemble each other – is still widely current.*

[19–21] How little . . . cruelty   *Portia loves Bassanio so much that she regards him as her own soul. Hence in saving Antonio (by buying him out of Shylock's clutches) she is 'redeeming' not only her husband's likeness but her own too.*

[25] husbandry and manage   *careful management*

[33] Not . . . imposition   *not to refuse this requirement of your services*

But if you knew to whom you show this honour,
How true a gentleman you send relief,
How dear a lover of my lord your husband,
I know you would be prouder of the work
Than customary bounty can enforce you.

PORTIA I never did repent for doing good,   10
Nor shall not now; for in companions
That do converse and waste the time together,
Whose souls do bear an equal yoke of love,
There must be needs a like proportion
Of lineaments, of manners, and of spirit;
Which makes me think that this Antonio,
Being the bosom lover of my lord,
Must needs be like my lord. If it be so,
How little is the cost I have bestowed
In purchasing the semblance of my soul   20
From out the state of hellish cruelty.
This comes too near the praising of myself,
Therefore no more of it. Hear other things –
Lorenzo, I commit into your hands
The husbandry and manage of my house
Until my lord's return. For mine own part,
I have toward heaven breathed a secret vow
To live in prayer and contemplation,
Only attended by Nerissa here,
Until her husband and my lord's return.   30
There is a monastery two miles off,
And there we will abide. I do desire you
Not to deny this imposition,
The which my love and some necessity
Now lays upon you.

LORENZO   Madam, with all my heart
I shall obey you in all fair commands.

[44] it back on you   *the same to you*

[46] ever   *always*

[48–9] And use . . . speed   *and go as fast as a man's legs will carry him*

[51] look   *look after*

[52] imagined speed   *all conceivable speed*
[53] traject   *the place where one boards 'the common ferry'*
[54] trades   *carries passengers*

[56] convenient speed   *speed befitting the occasion*

[60] a habit   *attire*
[61] accomplished   *equipped*
[62] With what we lack   *In young men's clothes, Portia and Nerissa will have to wear codpieces for the sake of authenticity.*
   hold thee any wager   *bet you anything you like*

PORTIA My people do already know my mind
 And will acknowledge you and Jessica
 In place of Lord Bassanio and myself.
 So fare you well till we shall meet again.   40
LORENZO Fair thoughts and happy hours attend on
 you!
JESSICA I wish your ladyship all heart's content.
PORTIA I thank you for your wish, and am well
 pleased
 To wish it back on you. Fare you well, Jessica.
     [*Exeunt* JESSICA *and* LORENZO
 [*Giving a letter*] Now, Balthasar,
 As I have ever found thee honest-true,
 So let me find thee still. Take this same letter,
 And use thou all th'endeavour of a man
 In speed to Padua. See thou render this
 Into my cousin's hand, Doctor Bellario,   50
 And look what notes and garments he doth give
 thee –
 Bring them, I pray thee, with imagined speed
 Unto the traject, to the common ferry
 Which trades to Venice. Waste no time in words
 But get thee gone. I shall be there before thee.
BALTHASAR Madam, I go with all convenient speed.
           [*Exit*
PORTIA Come on, Nerissa; I have work in hand
 That you yet know not of. We'll see our hus-
 bands
 Before they think of us!
NERISSA   Shall they see us?
PORTIA They shall, Nerissa, but in such a habit   60
 That they shall think we are accomplishèd
 With that we lack. I'll hold thee any wager,

[63] accoutered *dressed up*
[64] prettier *more stylish*
[65] the braver grace *more of a swagger*
[67] reed *squeaky*
    mincing steps *dainty steps (such as she takes now as a woman)*
[68] frays *fights, duels*
[69] Like a fine bragging youth *Portia's mocking picture of the male adolescent had a further humorous dimension in Shakespeare's theatre, where it was, of course, spoken by a boy acting a lady.*
    quaint *engagingly contrived*
[72] I could not do withal *as I could not (be bothered to) return their love*

[77] raw *immature*
    Jacks *fellows*
[78] turn to men. *change into men. (Portia, seeing a second possible sense of 'take men (to bed) as lovers', pretends to be shocked in her reply.)*
[81] device *plan*

ACT THREE, scene 5

This tedious brief scene, with its laboured humour, makes no contribution to the plot and, after the last scene, is hardly needed as 'light relief' before the trial. Originally, perhaps, it was inserted to allow Portia and Nerissa a fair time for their costume changing and to give the acting company's comedian a little more to do in the play.

[1–2] the sins . . . the children *He is giving Jessica a mock sermon and quoting part of the second of the Ten Commandments (on the consequences of worshipping false gods; Exodus 20:5).*
[3] I fear you *I fear for you (as you will surely go to hell)*
[4] agitation *He means 'cogitation' – considered opinion.*

When we are both accoutered like young men,
I'll prove the prettier fellow of the two,
And wear my dagger with the braver grace,
And speak between the change of man and boy
With a reed voice, and turn two mincing steps
Into a manly stride; and speak of frays
Like a fine bragging youth; and tell quaint lies
How honourable ladies sought my love, 70
Which I denying, they fell sick and died –
I could not do withal. Then I'll repent,
And wish, for all that, that I had not killed
them.
And twenty of these puny lies I'll tell,
That men shall swear I have discontinued
school
Above a twelvemonth. I have within my mind
A thousand raw tricks of these bragging Jacks,
Which I will practise.
NERISSA   Why, shall we turn to men?
PORTIA Fie, what a question's that,
If thou wert near a lewd interpreter! 80
But come, I'll tell thee all my whole device
When I am in my coach, which stays for us
At the park gate; and therefore haste away,
For we must measure twenty miles today.
                             [*Exeunt*

Scene 5. *Enter* LAUNCELOT (*the clown*) *and* JESSICA

LAUNCELOT Yes truly, for look you, the sins of the
father are to be laid upon the children. Therefore,
I promise you I fear you. I was always plain with
you, and so now I speak my agitation of the

[8] bastard   *both 'false' (hence deceitful) and 'illegitimate' (hence untenable)*

[11] got you not   *did not beget you*

[17–18] when I shun . . . your mother   *Scylla and Charybdis were legendary monsters. The first lived on a rock, the second by a whirlpool, at each side of dangerous straits between Italy and Sicily. Sailors who managed to avoid the one invariably fell into the clutches of the other.*

[20] saved by my husband   *In her turn Jessica argues from the Bible; see 1 Corinthians 7: 14.*

[23] enow   *enough*

[24] one by another   *together*

[24–7] This making . . . for money   *Jews don't eat pork; Christians do. Launcelot's foolish argument is that if too many people turn Christian there won't be enough pork to go round, and scarcity will bring soaring prices.*

[26–7] a rasher on the coals   *a broiled strip of bacon*

[31] get my wife into corners   *talk secretly with my wife (he implies that Launcelot is flirting with her)*

[33] are out   *have fallen out, have quarrelled*

matter. Therefore, be o' good cheer, for truly I
think you are damned. There is but one hope in
it that can do you any good, and that is but a kind
of bastard hope neither.

JESSICA And what hope is that, I pray thee?

LAUNCELOT Marry, you may partly hope that your 10
father got you not, that you are not the Jew's
daughter.

JESSICA That were a kind of bastard hope indeed!
So the sins of my mother should be visited upon
me.

LAUNCELOT Truly then I fear you are damned both
by father and mother. Thus when I shun Scylla
your father, I fall into Charybdis your mother.
Well, you are gone both ways.

JESSICA I shall be saved by my husband. He hath 20
made me a Christian.

LAUNCELOT Truly, the more to blame he! We were
Christians enow before, e'en as many as could
well live one by another. This making of Christians will raise the price of hogs; if we grow all to
be pork-eaters, we shall not shortly have a rasher
on the coals for money.

Enter LORENZO

JESSICA I'll tell my husband, Launcelot, what you
say. Here he comes.

LORENZO I shall grow jealous of you shortly, 30
Launcelot, if you thus get my wife into corners.

JESSICA Nay, you need not fear us, Lorenzo. Launcelot and I are out. He tells me flatly there's no
mercy for me in heaven because I am a Jew's

[39–41] the getting up . . . child by you *No doubt this was a topical joke when the play was first performed, but the exact reference is now a mystery. Lorenzo is accusing Launcelot of getting a Moorish woman pregnant. 'Moor' was pronounced 'more' – a fact from which Launcelot fashions a punning reply.*

[43] more than reason *bigger than is reasonable (by being pregnant)*

[43–4] if she be . . . I took her for *Somewhat gracelessly, Launcelot implies that 'the Moor' was only a common whore anyhow.*

[46–8] I think the best grace . . . parrots *Since fools who twist words out of their proper senses (as Launcelot has just done with 'Moor') bring speech itself into disrepute, talking will soon be a thing to admire only in parrots, and wise people will not speak at all.*

[51] stomachs *appetites*

[54–5] Only 'cover' is the word *The only thing still needed is the order to put the cloth on, and lay, the table.*

[57] Not so . . . duty *He quibbles on 'cover' meaning 'put your hat on' – something which it would be ill-mannered for him to do in the presence of his social superiors.*

[58] quarrelling with occasion *taking every chance to quibble*

[62] the table *In order to 'play upon the word' to the last Launcelot now takes 'table' in the sense of 'the food itself'.*

[65] covered *(in order to keep it hot)*

[66–7] as humours . . . govern *just as you please and fancy*

daughter; and he says you are no good member
of the commonwealth, for in converting Jews to
Christians you raise the price of pork.

LORENZO [*To* LAUNCELOT] I shall answer that better
to the commonwealth than you can the getting
up of the Negro's belly. The Moor is with child 40
by you, Launcelot.

LAUNCELOT It is much that the Moor should be
more than reason; but if she be less than an honest
woman, she is indeed more than I took her for.

LORENZO How every fool can play upon the word!
I think the best grace of wit will shortly turn into
silence, and discourse grow commendable in none
only but parrots. Go in, sirrah, bid them prepare
for dinner.

LAUNCELOT That is done, sir. They have all 50
stomachs.

LORENZO Goodly Lord, what a wit-snapper are you!
Then bid them prepare dinner.

LAUNCELOT That is done too, sir. Only 'cover' is the
word.

LORENZO Will you cover then, sir?

LAUNCELOT Not so, sir, neither. I know my duty.

LORENZO Yet more quarrelling with occasion! Wilt
thou show the whole wealth of thy wit in an
instant? I pray thee understand a plain man in his 60
plain meaning: go to thy fellows, bid them cover
the table, serve in the meat, and we will come in
to dinner.

LAUNCELOT For the table, sir, it shall be served in;
for the meat, sir, it shall be covered; for your
coming in to dinner, sir, why let it be as humours
and conceits shall govern. [*Exit*

[68] O dear ... suited (*One realises*) *how precious sound judgement is* (by) *seeing how* (ineptly) *he dresses matters up!*

[71] A many *numerous*

[72] Garnished like him *with a similar sprinkling of wit (or possibly 'clothed like him' since Launcelot may now be dressed in 'official' fool's motley)*

[72–3] for a tricksy word ... matter *for the sake of a showy bit of word-play scarcely make sense*

[73] How cheer'st thou, Jessica? *An affectionate inquiry changing the subject and delivered, no doubt, with a tender kiss.*

[76] meet *fitting*

[81] In reason *it is only reasonable that*

[83] on the wager lay *place as their bets*

[84–5] something else/Pawned *a further stake made*

[85] rude *rough*

[90] a stomach *both 'an appetite' (for dinner) and 'an inclination' (to praise you)*

[91] table-talk *conversation during our meal*

[93] I'll set you forth *I'll put you in your place (by what I find to say)*

LORENZO O dear discretion, how his words are
    suited!
    The fool hath planted in his memory
    An army of good words; and I do know   70
    A many fools that stand in better place,
    Garnished like him, that for a tricksy word
    Defy the matter. How cheer'st thou, Jessica?
    And now, good sweet, say thy opinion –
    How dost thou like the Lord Bassanio's wife?

JESSICA Past all expressing. It is very meet
    The Lord Bassanio live an upright life,
    For, having such a blessing in his lady,
    He finds the joys of heaven here on earth;
    And if on earth he do not merit it,   80
    In reason he should never come to heaven.
    Why, if two gods should play some heavenly
    match
    And on the wager lay two earthly women,
    And Portia one, there must be something else
    Pawned with the other, for the poor rude world
    Hath not her fellow.

LORENZO   Even such a husband
    Hast thou of me as she is for a wife.

JESSICA Nay, but ask my opinion too of that!

LORENZO I will anon. First let us go to dinner.

JESSICA Nay, let me praise you while I have a
    stomach.   90

LORENZO No, pray thee, let it serve for table-talk,
    Then howsome'er thou speak'st, 'mong other
    things
    I shall digest it.

JESSICA   Well, I'll set you forth.

                             [*Exeunt*

ACT FOUR, scene 1

The trial scene, the crux of the whole play, uses the full Elizabethan stage to present the Venetian court of justice. It may be supposed that Antonio, guarded, takes a place downstage, to one side, with his friends nearby; that the leading noblemen of Venice, magnificent in their dress as in name, sit in the gallery; that the Duke presides from a raised throne at the front of the inner stage, surrounded by officers and attendants. His formal, processional entry makes an imposing opening to the scene before a word is spoken.

[6] any dram   *even the merest scrap (literally, an eighth of a single ounce)*

[7] qualify   *moderate, soften*

[8] stands obdurate   *remains hard-hearted and unchangeable*

[10] out of his envy's reach   *out of range of his hatred*

[11] armed   *prepared*

[13] The very . . . his   *the oppressive and violent attack of his spirit*

[15]   *Shylock probably approaches from the upstage entrance diagonally opposite Antonio. On the Elizabethan stage, the door is a real one and Salerio calls out as it slowly begins to open.*

[16]   *The attendants who approached Shylock as he came in step back, leaving the Jew, isolated, to come to the centre of this Christian 'world'.*

[18–19] That thou . . . hour of act   *that you are only bringing this form of your hatred to the very brink of action*

[20] remorse more strange   *pity which is more wonderful*

[21] strange apparent   *peculiarly blatant*

ACT FOUR

Scene 1. *Enter the* DUKE, *the* MAGNIFICOES, OFFICERS *of the Court*, ANTONIO, BASSANIO, SALERIO *and* GRATIANO, *with other* ATTENDANTS

DUKE What, is Antonio here?

ANTONIO Ready, so please your Grace.

DUKE I am sorry for thee. Thou art come to answer
    A stony adversary, an inhuman wretch,
    Uncapable of pity, void and empty
    From any dram of mercy.

ANTONIO   I have heard
    Your Grace hath ta'en great pains to qualify
    His rigorous course; but since he stands ob-
       durate,
    And that no lawful means can carry me
    Out of his envy's reach, I do oppose   10
    My patience to his fury, and am armed
    To suffer with a quietness of spirit
    The very tyranny and rage of his.

DUKE Go one, and call the Jew into the court.

SALERIO He is ready at the door; he comes, my lord.

Enter SHYLOCK

DUKE Make room, and let him stand before our face.
    Shylock, the world thinks, and I think so too,
    That thou but lead'st this fashion of thy malice
    To the last hour of act; and then 'tis thought
    Thou'lt show thy mercy and remorse more
       strange   20
    Than is thy strange apparent cruelty;
    And where thou now exact'st the penalty,

THE MERCHANT OF VENICE

[24] loose the forfeiture *forgo your right to take Antonio's flesh*

[26] Forgive . . . principal *let him keep a part of the money he borrowed*

[29] enow *enough*

[30] commiseration of *compassion for*

[32] stubborn *unfeeling*

[32–3] never trained . . . courtesy *who have never been trained in kindly and considerate behaviour*

[34] expect *wait for*

      gentle *The pun here implies how his 'expectation' is about to be disappointed. Shylock is no gentile, and will give no gentle answer.*

[35] possessed *informed*

      purpose *intend*

[38–9] If you deny it . . . freedom! *Compare III. 2. 278–80 and III. 3. 27–31. Shylock implies that the court's decision against him would directly flout the principle of racial tolerance on which Venice was founded.*

[41] carrion *A term of contempt – 'rotten'.*

[43] it is my humour *because I choose to. This is indeed no answer! By his 'humour' he means his 'whim' – there is no sense of amusement in the word here. His speech is now directed at the court as a whole – and at Antonio and his supporters in particular – not just at the Duke.*

[46] baned *poisoned*

[47] a gaping pig *A roasted pig was often served with fruit stuffed in its open mouth.*

[49] sings i'th'nose *drones*

[50–52] for affection . . . loathes *because likes and dislikes that are inborn determine the bent of our emotions and stronger feelings (a specious argument for prejudice as a natural phenomenon)*

Which is a pound of this poor merchant's flesh,
Thou wilt not only loose the forfeiture,
But, touched with human gentleness and love,
Forgive a moiety of the principal –
Glancing an eye of pity on his losses
That have of late so huddled on his back,
Enow to press a royal merchant down
And pluck commiseration of his state   30
From brassy bosoms and rough hearts of flint,
From stubborn Turks and Tartars never trained
To offices of tender courtesy.
We all expect a gentle answer, Jew.

SHYLOCK I have possessed your Grace of what I purpose,
And by our holy Sabbath have I sworn
To have the due and forfeit of my bond.
If you deny it, let the danger light
Upon your charter and your city's freedom!
You'll ask me why I rather choose to have   40
A weight of carrion flesh than to receive
Three thousand ducats. I'll not answer that,
But say it is my humour. Is it answered?
What if my house be troubled with a rat,
And I be pleased to give ten thousand ducats
To have it baned? What, are you answered yet?
Some men there are love not a gaping pig,
Some that are mad if they behold a cat,
And others, when the bagpipe sings i'th'nose,
Cannot contain their urine; for affection,   50
Master of passion, sways it to the mood
Of what it likes or loathes. Now for your answer:

[54, 55, 56] he . . . he . . . he *the one man . . . the other . . . and the other*

[56] woollen *The bag of the instrument was often wrapped in woollen material.*

[56–7] of force/Must *each is bound to*

[58] As to . . . offended *as to give offence to others in the way he responds to what he finds offensive*

[60] lodged *fixed*

    certain *special. Compare I. 3. 43–53.*

[62] A losing suit *To gain his pound of flesh he is losing three thousand ducats.*

[63–4] *The purpose of Shylock's 'answer' was not to explain but to taunt – most successfully, as the exchange with Bassanio demonstrates.*

[68] a hate at first *an immediate cause for hate*

[70] think you . . . the Jew *remember you are arguing with Shylock*

[72] bid the main flood bate *ask the high tide not to reach*

[76] and to *and bid them to*

[77] fretten with *tossed by*

As there is no firm reason to be rendered
Why he cannot abide a gaping pig,
Why he a harmless necessary cat,
Why he a woollen bagpipe, but of force
Must yield to such inevitable shame
As to offend, himself being offended –
So can I give no reason, nor I will not,
More than a lodged hate and a certain loathing   60
I bear Antonio, that I follow thus
A losing suit against him. Are you answered?

BASSANIO This is no answer, thou unfeeling man,
To excuse the current of thy cruelty!

SHYLOCK I am not bound to please thee with my
answers.

BASSANIO Do all men kill the things they do not love?

SHYLOCK Hates any man the thing he would not kill?

BASSANIO Every offence is not a hate at first.

SHYLOCK What, wouldst thou have a serpent sting
thee twice?

ANTONIO I pray you, think you question with the
Jew.   70
You may as well go stand upon the beach
And bid the main flood bate his usual height;
You may as well use question with the wolf
Why he hath made the ewe bleat for the lamb;
You may as well forbid the mountain pines
To wag their high tops and to make no noise
When they are fretten with the gusts of heaven;
You may as well do anything most hard
As seek to soften that – than which what's
harder? –
His Jewish heart. Therefore I do beseech you   80
Make no more offers, use no farther means,

[82] with all . . . conveniency *with proper straightforwardness* (*Antonio sees that argument is futile and merely prolongs his agony*)

[85–7] *compare III. 2. 285–9*

[89] What judgement . . . wrong? *The whole of Shylock's 'case' in a nutshell. It is a shocking question because it assumes that 'doing right' and 'doing wrong' are merely matters of legal judgement.*

[92] in abject . . . parts *for menial tasks*

[97] Be seasoned . . . viands *be treated to the same food (as yours)*

[98] So do I answer you. *This 'answer' addresses the feelings (as Shylock's answer at III. 1. 74–6 does) but the thought behind it is (again) feeble. In the analogy between paying-to-own-slaves and paying-to-put-a-man-to-death the two 'wrongs' are not equally severe.*

[100] dearly bought *see [62]*

[103] *No doubt there is a long pause before the Duke speaks. In Shylock's terms no answer can be given: and an answer in any other terms will clearly have no effect on his righteous and fervid malevolence.*

[104] Upon my power *I have the authority to*

[105–7] *Through this coincidence with Portia's plans in III. 4, Shakespeare takes a short cut, and keeps up his pace, in the plot.*

[107] stays without *waits outside*

But with all brief and plain conveniency
Let me have judgement, and the Jew his will.

BASSANIO [*To* SHYLOCK] For thy three thousand
    ducats here is six.

SHYLOCK If every ducat in six thousand ducats
    Were in six parts, and every part a ducat,
    I would not draw them. I would have my bond.

DUKE How shalt thou hope for mercy, rendering
    none?

SHYLOCK What judgement shall I dread, doing no
    wrong?
    You have among you many a purchased slave,   90
    Which like your asses and your dogs and mules
    You use in abject and in slavish parts,
    Because you bought them. Shall I say to you,
    'Let them be free – marry them to your heirs!
    Why sweat they under burdens? Let their beds
    Be made as soft as yours, and let their palates
    Be seasoned with such viands'? You will answer,
    'The slaves are ours.' So do I answer you.
    The pound of flesh which I demand of him
    Is dearly bought, 'tis mine, and I will have it. 100
    If you deny me, fie upon your law!
    There is no force in the decrees of Venice.
    I stand for judgement. Answer – shall I have
    it?

DUKE Upon my power I may dismiss this court
    Unless Bellario, a learnèd doctor
    Whom I have sent for to determine this,
    Come here today.

SALERIO   My lord, here stays without
    A messenger with letters from the doctor,
    New come from Padua.

[110] Call the messenger   *No doubt Salerio, or an attendant, does as he is told and goes to the door to call Nerissa into court.*

[112–13] The Jew . . . blood   *Bassanio means this not literally but as an expression of the sincerity of his friendship (and, as such, it is more convincing in performance than when read).*

[114] a tainted wether   *a sick ram (strictly speaking, a castrated – and hence impotent – ram)*

[115] Meetest   *fittest*

[118] live still   *go on living*

[Enter Nerissa dressed like a lawyer's clerk]   *In the Elizabethan theatre, the disguise, like Portia's, is all the more convincing for 'her' being in fact a boy!*

[She presents a letter]   *While the Duke reads to himself, Shylock starts to sharpen his knife (and the pun at l. 123 shows precisely how).*

[121]   *This action, like all Shylock has said in the court, is intended to bait the Christians – and this time Gratiano 'rises to it' (compare l. 63).*

[125] hangman's   *executioner's (usually a hangman was a headsman too)*

[126] envy   *malicious hatred*

[128] inexcrable   *thoroughly abominable (possibly an error for 'inexorable', meaning 'relentless and not to be moved by prayers')*

[129] And . . . accused!   *the fact that you exist makes one question the existence of justice*

DUKE Bring us the letters. Call the messenger.   110
BASSANIO Good cheer, Antonio. What, man, courage
    yet!
    The Jew shall have my flesh, blood, bones, and
        all,
    Ere thou shalt lose for me one drop of blood.
ANTONIO I am a tainted wether of the flock,
    Meetest for death. The weakest kind of fruit
    Drops earliest to the ground, and so let me.
    You cannot better be employed, Bassanio,
    Than to live still, and write mine epitaph.

Enter NERISSA, *dressed like a lawyer's clerk*

DUKE Came you from Padua, from Bellario?
NERISSA From both, my lord. Bellario greets your
    Grace.   120

She presents a letter

BASSANIO [*To* SHYLOCK] Why dost thou whet thy
    knife so earnestly?
SHYLOCK To cut the forfeiture from that bankrupt
    there.
GRATIANO Not on thy sole, but on thy soul, harsh
    Jew,
    Thou mak'st thy knife keen; but no metal can –
    No, not the hangman's axe – bear half the
    keenness
    Of thy sharp envy. Can no prayers pierce thee?
SHYLOCK No, none that thou hast wit enough to
    make.
GRATIANO O be thou damned, inexecrable dog,
    And for thy life let justice be accused!
    Thou almost mak'st me waver in my faith,   130

[131] **Pythagoras** *This Greek philosopher's theory of the 'trans-migration' of souls from dead animals to men is not compatible with Christian belief (l. 130).*

[134] **a wolf ... slaughter** *Captured killer animals were some-times destroyed by hanging. (The Latin for 'wolf' is 'lupus'. There may thus be a topical reference intended – to Dr Lopez, a Portuguese Jew who was hanged in London in June 1594. He was the Queen's physician and had been accused of trying to poison her.)*

[135] **fell** *savage*
      fleet *speed away*
[136] **unhallowed dam** *unholy mother*
[139] **rail** *scold*

[140] **Thou ... lungs** *you merely hurt your lungs*

To hold opinion with Pythagoras
That souls of animals infuse themselves
Into the trunks of men. Thy currish spirit
Governed a wolf, who hanged for human
    slaughter –
Even from the gallows did his fell soul fleet,
And whilst thou layest in thy unhallowed dam,
Infused itself in thee; for thy desires
Are wolvish, bloody, starved, and ravenous.

SHYLOCK Till thou canst rail the seal from off my
    bond,
Thou but offend'st thy lungs to speak so loud. 140
Repair thy wit, good youth, or it will fall
To cureless ruin. I stand here for law.

DUKE This letter from Bellario doth commend
A young and learnèd doctor to our court.
Where is he?

NERISSA   He attendeth here hard by
To know your answer whether you'll admit
    him.

DUKE With all my heart. Some three or four of you
Go give him courteous conduct to this place.

              [*Exeunt several* ATTENDANTS
Meantime the court shall hear Bellario's letter.
[*Reads*] *Your Grace shall understand that at the* 150
receipt of your letter I am very sick; but in the
instant that your messenger came, in loving visita-
tion was with me a young doctor of Rome. His name
is Balthasar. I acquainted him with the cause in
controversy between the Jew and Antonio the mer-
chant. We turned o'er many books together. He is
furnished with my opinion which (bettered with his
own learning, the greatness whereof I cannot

179

THE MERCHANT OF VENICE

[159] at my importunity   *on my urging*

[161–2] let his lack . . . estimation   *do not treat him any the less respectfully on account of his youth*

[164] whose trial . . . commendation   *and his conduct of this case will show you his worth even better (than my words)*

[169] take your place   *Since she embodies the 'judgement' that Shylock called for at l. 103, her 'place' is a central one, facing the audience, with Nerissa 'clerking' nearby, and Antonio and Shylock downstage on opposite sides.*

[170] the difference . . . the court   *the quarrel that gives rise to this trial*

[172] throughly   *thoroughly*
      cause   *case*

[177] in such rule   *it is so correctly conducted*

[178] Cannot . . . proceed   *cannot rebut the charge you are making*

[179] within his danger   *in his power to harm*

enough commend) comes with him at my importunity
to fill up your Grace's request in my stead. I beseech 160
you let his lack of years be no impediment to let him
lack a reverend estimation, for I never knew so
young a body with so old a head. I leave him to your
gracious acceptance, whose trial shall better publish
his commendation.

Enter PORTIA *as Balthasar, dressed like a*
Doctor of Laws

You hear the learn'd Bellario, what he writes;
And here, I take it, is the doctor come.
[*To* PORTIA] Give me your hand. Come you
    from old Bellario?

PORTIA I did, my lord.

DUKE   You are welcome; take your place.
Are you acquainted with the difference   170
That holds this present question in the
    court?

PORTIA I am informèd throughly of the cause.
Which is the merchant here? And which the
    Jew?

DUKE Antonio and old Shylock, both stand forth.

PORTIA Is your name Shylock?

SHYLOCK   Shylock is my name.

PORTIA Of a strange nature is the suit you follow,
Yet in such rule that the Venetian law
Cannot impugn you as you do proceed.
[*To* ANTONIO] You stand within his danger, do
    you not?

ANTONIO Ay, so he says.

PORTIA   Do you confess the bond?   180

ANTONIO I do.

THE MERCHANT OF VENICE

[181] Then ... merciful *The line is like a veiled warning:*
'Then it would be best for the Jew to be merciful' ...

[182] ... *but Shylock hears, and resents, it as an order.*

[183] strained *forced, constrained*

[185] the place beneath *Since the roof over the Elizabethan
stage was known as 'heaven', a specific 'place beneath' is also evoked
here – the scene itself.*

blest *endowed with power to bless*

[186] It blesseth ... takes *mercy does good both to those who
show it and to those who receive it*

[187] becomes *suits*

[188] The thronèd monarch *The Duke of Venice sits 'thronèd'
in the background of this speech.*

[189] temporal *earthly (as opposed to divine)*

[190] The attribute to *(the force of temporal power is) the
sustaining quality.*

[191] Wherein ... kings *which makes men frightened of kings*

[196] seasons *tempers, leavens*

[198–9] That in ... salvation *if God showed us nothing but
justice we would all be condemned, since we are all sinners*

[201] *Although Portia's great speech refers clearly to Christian
belief (and notably to the Lord's Prayer here) it is not exclusively
Christian. In most religions men 'pray for mercy'. She aims to lift
Shylock's concern for mere legality to the level of religious principle;
and she meets with a signal lack of success (l. 205).*

[202] mitigate *moderate, soften*

[205] *In this context, Shylock's blunt rejection of Portia's appeal to
divine sanctions, his preference for his own dreadful 'temporal power'
over his enemy, has something of the force of blasphemy. In one sense
he damns himself from now on.*

[209] Yea, twice the sum *see l. 84*

I will be bound *I will swear according to the law*

PORTIA   Then must the Jew be merciful.
SHYLOCK On what compulsion must I? Tell me that.
PORTIA The quality of mercy is not strained;
          It droppeth as the gentle rain from heaven
          Upon the place beneath. It is twice blest;
          It blesseth him that gives and him that takes.
          'Tis mightiest in the mightiest; it becomes
          The thronèd monarch better than his crown.
          His sceptre shows the force of temporal power,
          The attribute to awe and majesty,   190
          Wherein doth sit the dread and fear of kings;
          But mercy is above this sceptred sway,
          It is enthronèd in the hearts of kings,
          It is an attribute to God himself,
          And earthly power doth then show likest God's
          When mercy seasons justice. Therefore, Jew,
          Though justice be thy plea, consider this –
          That in the course of justice none of us
          Should see salvation. We do pray for mercy,
          And that same prayer doth teach us all to render 200
          The deeds of mercy. I have spoke thus much
          To mitigate the justice of thy plea,
          Which if thou follow, this strict court of Venice
          Must needs give sentence 'gainst the merchant-
               there.
SHYLOCK My deeds upon my head! I crave the law,
          The penalty and forfeit of my bond.
PORTIA Is he not able to discharge the money?
BASSANIO Yes, here I tender it for him in the court,
          Yea, twice the sum. If that will not suffice,
          I will be bound to pay it ten times o'er   210
          On forfeit of my hands, my head, my heart.
          If this will not suffice, it must appear

[213] malice bears down truth *hatred is oppressing sincerity.* (*An exact summary of the situation on the stage.*)

[214] Wrest . . . authority *just for once use your position to twist the law*

[222] Daniel *A devout young man who judged wisely and confounded the corrupt Elders in the story of Susannah (in the Apocrypha).*

[227] An oath *see I. 3. 43–53*

[228] perjury upon my soul? (*by wilfully going against a sworn intention?*)

[232] Nearest the merchant's heart *see note on III. 1. 131*

[234] according to the tenour *precisely as specified therein*

[236–7] your exposition . . . most sound *Her speech on 'the quality of mercy' has gone right out of his mind since she declared the law's apparent support for his case.*

[241] I stay here on my bond *see note on III. 3. 17*

That malice bears down truth. And I beseech
    you,
Wrest once the law to your authority.
To do a great right do a little wrong,
And curb this cruel devil of his will.

PORTIA It must not be. There is no power in Venice
    Can alter a decree establishèd.
    'Twill be recorded for a precedent,
    And many an error by the same example   220
    Will rush into the state. It cannot be.

SHYLOCK A Daniel come to judgement! Yea, a
    Daniel!
    O wise young judge, how I do honour thee!

PORTIA I pray you let me look upon the bond.

SHYLOCK Here 'tis, most reverend doctor, here it is.

PORTIA [*After reading the bond*] Shylock, there's
    thrice thy money offered thee.

SHYLOCK An oath, an oath! I have an oath in heaven;
    Shall I lay perjury upon my soul?
    No, not for Venice!

PORTIA   Why, this bond is forfeit,
    And lawfully by this the Jew may claim   230
    A pound of flesh, to be by him cut off
    Nearest the merchant's heart. Be merciful;
    Take thrice thy money; bid me tear the bond.

SHYLOCK When it is paid, according to the tenour.
    It doth appear you are a worthy judge,
    You know the law, your exposition
    Hath been most sound. I charge you by the law,
    Whereof you are a well-deserving pillar,
    Proceed to judgement. By my soul I swear
    There is no power in the tongue of man   240
    To alter me. I stay here on my bond.

[242–3] Most heartily . . . judgement *See l. 280 and compare ll. 80–3. The pun makes the strain that Antonio is undergoing uncomfortably clear.*

[247] Hath full relation to *fully endorses*

[254] balance *A plural noun, 'scales'.*

[255] I have them ready. *By a telling visual 'pun', as Shylock holds the scales up, with his knife raised in his other hand, he is shown to the audience to be a mockery (figure) of Justice.*
[256] Have by some *call in a*
    on your charge *at your expense*

[261] *This cold-blooded rejoinder makes* manifest *the fact that Shylock is seeking Antonio's* life *(and not just some of his flesh). See l. 357*
[263] I am armed *my spirit is ready (to face death)*

[267] still her use *her habit*

ANTONIO Most heartily I do beseech the court
    To give the judgement.
PORTIA   Why then, thus it is:
    You must prepare your bosom for his knife.
SHYLOCK O noble judge! O excellent young man!
PORTIA For the intent and purpose of the law
    Hath full relation to the penalty,
    Which here appeareth due upon the bond.
SHYLOCK 'Tis very true. O wise and upright judge,
    How much more elder art thou than thy looks! 250
PORTIA Therefore lay bare your bosom.
SHYLOCK   Ay, his breast,
    So says the bond, doth it not, noble judge?
    'Nearest his heart' – those are the very words.
PORTIA It is so. Are there balance here to weigh
    The flesh?
SHYLOCK   I have them ready.
PORTIA Have by some surgeon, Shylock, on your
    charge,
    To stop his wounds, lest he do bleed to death.
SHYLOCK Is it so nominated in the bond?
PORTIA It is not so expressed, but what of that?
    'Twere good you do so much for charity.   260

SHYLOCK *takes the bond from her*

SHYLOCK I cannot find it; 'tis not in the bond.
PORTIA You, merchant, have you anything to say?
ANTONIO But little. I am armed and well prepared.
    Give me your hand, Bassanio; fare you well.
    Grieve not that I am fallen to this for you;
    For herein Fortune shows herself more kind
    Than is her custom. It is still her use
    To let the wretched man outlive his wealth,

[271] she   *Fortune*

[274] speak me fair in death   *speak well of the way I died (or
'speak kindly of me when I am dead')*

[275] bid her be judge   *She is, of course, 'being judge' even as he
speaks! And her 'judgement' on the depth of friendship between
Antonio and Bassanio follows (l. 287).*

[277] Repent but you   *only show your regret*

[280]   *A brave, wry, deliberate pun that epitomises how differently
Antonio is bound to Shylock and to Bassanio.*

[281] Antonio . . . to deliver you   *see [112-13]*

[287-93] Your wife . . . unquiet house   *For the audience, the
humour and dramatic irony here briefly relieve the accumulating
tension of the scene, just before its climax.*

[294-6] These be . . . a Christian   *The lines blend Shylock's
fanatical hatred with a reminder of his pain (so that, even on the brink
of murder, he is not utterly despicable to the audience).*

[295] Barabbas   *The name of the thief and murderer who was
released to the Jews when Christ was crucified; and the name of 'The
Jew of Malta' in Marlowe's play of that title, a villain-hero.*

To view with hollow eye and wrinkled brow
An age of poverty; from which lingering
    penance   270
Of such misery doth she cut me off.
Commend me to your honourable wife,
Tell her the process of Antonio's end,
Say how I loved you, speak me fair in death;
And when the tale is told, bid her be judge
Whether Bassanio had not once a love.
Repent but you that you shall lose your friend,
And he repents not that he pays your debt;
For if the Jew do cut but deep enough,
I'll pay it instantly with all my heart.   280
BASSANIO Antonio, I am married to a wife
  Which is as dear to me as life itself;
  But life itself, my wife, and all the world
  Are not with me esteemed above thy life.
  I would lose all, ay sacrifice them all
  Here to this devil, to deliver you.
PORTIA Your wife would give you little thanks for
    that
  If she were by to hear you make the offer.
GRATIANO I have a wife who I protest I love –
  I would she were in heaven, so she could   290
  Entreat some power to change this currish Jew.
NERISSA 'Tis well you offer it behind her back,
  The wish would make else an unquiet house.
SHYLOCK [*Aside*] These be the Christian husbands!
    I have a daughter;
  Would any of the stock of Barabbas
  Had been her husband, rather than a Christian.
  [*To* PORTIA] We trifle time. I pray thee pursue
    sentence.

[298–302] *The two parts of her 'sentence' are matched in their formal cadence, pivoting on the words, 'Most rightful judge' and aurally imaging the 'balance' of unmitigated justice.*

[303–4] Come, prepare!/Tarry a little *As he advances on Antonio, knife raised in savage eagerness to kill, Portia's words 'freeze' him for a moment, fixing the murderous intention in the eye of all spectators.*

[306] The words expressly are *Now she makes* her *stand on 'the letter of the law' – exactly as Shylock has done . . .*

[312] *. . . and Gratiano exults in gloating outcry – exactly as Shylock has done.*

PORTIA A pound of that same merchant's flesh is
 thine.
 The court awards it, and the law doth give it.
SHYLOCK Most rightful judge!   300
PORTIA And you must cut this flesh from off his
 breast.
 The law allows it, and the court awards it.
SHYLOCK Most learnèd judge! A sentence! Come,
 prepare!
PORTIA Tarry a little – there is something else.
 This bond doth give thee here no jot of blood;
 The words expressly are 'a pound of flesh'.
 Take then thy bond, take thou thy pound of
 flesh;
 But in the cutting it, if thou dost shed
 One drop of Christian blood, thy lands and
 goods
 Are by the laws of Venice confiscate   310
 Unto the state of Venice.
GRATIANO O upright judge! Mark, Jew. O learned
 judge!
SHYLOCK Is that the law?
PORTIA   Thyself shall see the act;
 For, as thou urgest justice, be assured
 Thou shalt have justice more than thou desir'st.
GRATIANO O learned judge. Mark, Jew. A learned
 judge!
SHYLOCK I take this offer then. Pay the bond thrice
 And let the Christian go.
BASSANIO   Here is the money.
PORTIA Soft!
 The Jew shall have all justice. Soft, no haste, 320
 He shall have nothing but the penalty.

[325–30] But . . . hair *by even the weight of a hair. The imagery of diminishing weight emphasises the evaporation of Shylock's power.*
[327–9] in the substance . . . poor scruple *to the extent of a grain (the tiniest measure in the apothecaries' scale of weights) or a fraction of a grain*

[333] on the hip *compare Shylock at I. 3. 47–8*

[335] principal *just the money lent (that is, three thousand ducats)*

[339] a second Daniel *The comparison is apt enough, for Daniel confounded the Elders by turning their own words against them.*

[345] question *to argue the matter*
[346] *Presumably Portia has acquired her knowledge of stern and obscure Venetian law from Bellario.*

[351] contrive *plot*

GRATIANO O Jew! An upright judge, a learned
    judge!

PORTIA Therefore prepare thee to cut off the flesh.
    Shed thou no blood, nor cut thou less nor more
    But just a pound of flesh. If thou tak'st more
    Or less than a just pound, be it but so much
    As makes it light or heavy in the substance
    Or the division of the twentieth part
    Of one poor scruple, nay, if the scale do turn
    But in the estimation of a hair,   330
    Thou diest, and all thy goods are confiscate.

GRATIANO A second Daniel! A Daniel, Jew!
    Now, infidel, I have you on the hip!

PORTIA Why doth the Jew pause? Take thy for-
    feiture.

SHYLOCK Give me my principal, and let me go.

BASSANIO I have it ready for thee; here it is.

PORTIA He hath refused it in the open court.
    He shall have merely justice and his bond.

GRATIANO A Daniel still say I, a second Daniel!
    I thank thee, Jew, for teaching me that word.   340

SHYLOCK Shall I not have barely my principal?

PORTIA Thou shalt have nothing but the forfeiture,
    To be so taken at thy peril, Jew.

SHYLOCK Why, then the devil give him good of it!
    I'll stay no longer question.

PORTIA   Tarry Jew!
    The law hath yet another hold on you.
    It is enacted in the laws of Venice,
    If it be proved against an alien
    That by direct or indirect attempts
    He seek the life of any citizen,   350
    The party 'gainst the which he doth contrive

[353] privy coffer of the state *the treasury of Venice*

[354–5] And . . . voice *and the offender is condemned to death unless the Duke reprieve him (and no one else may do so)*

[357] manifest proceeding *see l. 253 and l. 261*

[361] The danger . . . rehearsed *the punishment that I have just declared*

[363] *The Jew-baiting that Gratiano indulges in now is as ugly as any of Shylock's Christian-baiting earlier in the scene.*

[370–1] The other half . . . fine *the seizure of the other half of your wealth may take the lighter form of a fine, if you show a proper humility*

[372] for *for the benefit of*

[378] A halter gratis *a noose, free of charge (to hang himself in)*

Shall seize one half his goods, the other half
Comes to the privy coffer of the state,
And the offender's life lies in the mercy
Of the Duke only, 'gainst all other voice.
In which predicament I say thou stand'st;
For it appears by manifest proceeding
That indirectly, and directly too,
Thou hast contrived against the very life
Of the defendant; and thou hast incurred   360
The danger formerly by me rehearsed.
Down therefore, and beg mercy of the Duke.

SHYLOCK *falls to his knees*

GRATIANO Beg that thou mayst have leave to hang
   thyself –
   And yet, thy wealth being forfeit to the state,
   Thou hast not left the value of a cord,
   Therefore thou must be hanged at the state's
   charge.
DUKE That thou shalt see the difference of our spirit,
   I pardon thee thy life before thou ask it.
   For half thy wealth, it is Antonio's;
   The other half comes to the general state,   370
   Which humbleness may drive unto a fine.
PORTIA Ay, for the state, not for Antonio.
SHYLOCK Nay, take my life and all! Pardon not that!
   You take my house when you do take the prop
   That doth sustain my house. You take my life
   When you do take the means whereby I live.
PORTIA What mercy can you render him, Antonio?
GRATIANO A halter gratis! Nothing else, for God's
   sake!

THE MERCHANT OF VENICE

[380] quit *release Shylock from*

[382] in use *in trust (Antonio's proposal is that he should administer his half of Shylock's estate for the benefit of Lorenzo and Jessica, not for personal profit – a generous idea, since Antonio himself is poverty-stricken)*

[386] presently *immediately*
       become a Christian *Such compulsory conversion, backed by Antonio's second proviso and enforced by the Duke (l. 390), seems hardly an act of mercy.*
[388] all he dies possessed *everything he owns by the time he dies*
[390] recant *withdraw*

[397] two godfathers *(as is the custom at baptism). But 'god-fathers' was also a joking word for jurymen and . . .*

[398] ten more *. . . Gratiano wishes a twelve-man jury had condemned Shylock to death instead.*

ANTONIO So please my lord the Duke and all the
    court
      To quit the fine for one half of his goods,   380
      I am content, so he will let me have
      The other half in use, to render it
      Upon his death unto the gentleman
      That lately stole his daughter.
      Two things provided more: that for this favour
      He presently become a Christian;
      The other, that he do record a gift
      Here in the court of all he dies possessed
      Unto his son Lorenzo and his daughter.

DUKE He shall do this, or else I do recant   390
    The pardon that I late pronouncèd here.

PORTIA Art thou contented, Jew? What dost thou say?

SHYLOCK I am content.

PORTIA [*To* NERISSA]   Clerk, draw a deed of gift.

SHYLOCK [*Rising*] I pray you give me leave to go
    from hence.
    I am not well – send the deed after me,
    And I will sign it.

DUKE   Get thee gone, but do it.

GRATIANO In christ'ning shalt thou have two god-
    fathers.
    Had I been judge, thou shouldst have had ten
    more,
    To bring thee to the gallows, not to the font.
                    [*Exit* SHYLOCK

DUKE [*To* PORTIA] Sir, I entreat you home with me
    to dinner.   400

PORTIA I humbly do desire your Grace of pardon.
    I must away this night toward Padua,
    And it is meet I presently set forth.

[404] your leisure serves you not   *you have not more time at your disposal*

[405] gratify   *show your gratitude to*

[406] much bound   *greatly indebted*

[Exit Duke and his train]   *The court empties, and the curtains are probably drawn closed across the inner stage by one of the attendants, marking the 'change of key' in the scene. Antonio, Bassanio, Gratiano, Portia and Nerissa are left alone on stage, the ladies seeking to avoid too prolonged a confrontation lest their disguises be seen through at close quarters.*

[409] in lieu whereof   *in return for this (service)*

[411] We freely . . . withal   *we most willingly give you in reward for your kind efforts on our behalf*

[417] My mind . . . mercenary   *I have never been more money-minded than that*

[418] I pray you . . . again   *A polite commonplace, the equivalent of 'Here's to the next time', which Portia uses with mischievous irony.*

[420] of force . . . further   *I really must try again to persuade you*

[425] for your sake   *to acknowledge your politeness*

[426] for your love   *to acknowledge your friendship (over and above politeness)*

this ring   *It caught her eye, no doubt, as Bassanio handed her the gloves.*

DUKE I am sorry that your leisure serves you not.
    Antonio, gratify this gentleman,
      For in my mind you are much bound to him.

                       [*Exit* DUKE *and his train*

BASSANIO [*To* PORTIA] Most worthy gentleman, I
    and my friend
    Have by your wisdom been this day acquitted
    Of grievous penalties; in lieu whereof,
    Three thousand ducats due unto the Jew   410
    We freely cope your courteous pains withal.

ANTONIO And stand indebted, over and above,
    In love and service to you evermore.

PORTIA He is well paid that is well satisfied,
    And I delivering you am satisfied,
    And therein do account myself well paid;
    My mind was never yet more mercenary.
    I pray you know me when we meet again.
    I wish you well, and so I take my leave.

BASSANIO Dear sir, of force I must attempt you
    further.   420
    Take some remembrance of us as a tribute,
    Not as a fee. Grant me two things, I pray you –
    Not to deny me, and to pardon me.

PORTIA You press me far, and therefore I will yield.
    Give me your gloves; I'll wear them for your
    sake –

                BASSANIO *hands her his gloves*

    And for your love I'll take this ring from you.
    Do not draw back your hand; I'll take no more,
    And you in love shall not deny me this.

BASSANIO This ring, good sir? Alas, it is a trifle!
    I will not shame myself to give you this.   430

[432] And now . . . it   *and indeed I am really drawn to it now*
[433] the value   *the mere cost of the ring*

[435] by proclamation   *by public announcement (that I wish to buy it)*
[436] Only . . . me   *but in the case of this ring, please excuse me*

[443] 'scuse   *excuse*

[446] hold out enemy   *stay angry with you*

[450] valued 'gainst   *valued even more highly than*

PORTIA I will have nothing else but only this –
    And now methinks I have a mind to it.
BASSANIO There's more depends on this than on the
    value.
    The dearest ring in Venice will I give you,
    And find it out by proclamation.
    Only for this, I pray you pardon me.
PORTIA I see, sir, you are liberal in offers.
    You taught me first to beg, and now methinks
    You teach me how a beggar should be answered.
BASSANIO Good sir, this ring was given me by my
    wife,   440
    And when she put it on she made me vow
    That I should neither sell, nor give, nor lose it.
PORTIA That 'scuse serves many men to save their
    gifts –
    And if your wife be not a mad woman,
    And know how well I have deserved this ring,
    She would not hold out enemy for ever
    For giving it to me. Well, peace be with you!
                        [*Exeunt* PORTIA *and* NERISSA
ANTONIO My Lord Bassanio, let him have the ring.
    Let his deservings, and my love withal,
    Be valued 'gainst your wife's commandèment. 450
BASSANIO Go, Gratiano, run and overtake him;
    Give him the ring and bring him if thou canst
    Unto Antonio's house. Away, make haste!
                        [*Exit* GRATIANO
    [*To* ANTONIO] Come, you and I will thither
    presently,
    And in the morning early will we both
    Fly toward Belmont. Come, Antonio.
                            [*Exeunt*

ACT FOUR, scene 2

*The action flows straight on, as the joke expands predictably.
Portia and Nerissa, having made their last exit on one side,
have crossed the backstage and now appear from the other.*

[1] this deed   *the deed of gift for Lorenzo* (IV. 1. 393)
[4] This deed   *both 'Shylock's legacy' and 'our action'* (*in
wringing it out of him*)

[15] old   *abundant, ample*

Scene 2. *Enter* PORTIA *and* NERISSA, *disguised as before*

PORTIA Inquire the Jew's house out, give him this
    deed,
    And let him sign it. We'll away tonight
    And be a day before our husbands home.
    This deed will be well welcome to Lorenzo.

Enter GRATIANO

GRATIANO Fair sir, you are well o'erta'en.
    My Lord Bassanio upon more advice
    Hath sent you here this ring, and doth entreat
    Your company at dinner.
PORTIA   That cannot be.
    His ring I do accept most thankfully,
    And so I pray you tell him. Furthermore,   10
    I pray you show my youth old Shylock's house.
GRATIANO That will I do.
NERISSA [*To* PORTIA] Sir, I would speak with you.
    [*Aside to* PORTIA] I'll see if I can get my
        husband's ring,
    Which I did make him swear to keep for ever.
PORTIA [*Aside to* NERISSA] Thou mayst, I warrant.
    We shall have old swearing
    That they did give the rings away to men;
    But we'll outface them, and outswear them too.
    [*Aloud*] Away, make haste. Thou know'st
        where I will tarry.
NERISSA [*To* GRATIANO] Come, good sir, will you
    show me to this house?   20
                    [*Exeunt*

ACT FIVE, scene 1

A certain determined playfulness stays in the air, blended with some romantic indulgence, as the spirit of 'an eye for an eye' in Venice gives way to the practice of lovers' 'tit for tat' in the garden at Belmont.

[Enter Lorenzo and Jessica]   *Perhaps they come from the inner stage, half opening its curtains to suggest the 'hall' of Portia's house; or they may come from one of the two side doors, leaving the other to be used by all the characters who arrive from Venice in this scene.*

[1]   In such a night   *The phrase, repeated seven times in the next twenty lines, works like a refrain in a song to 'point' the audience's imagination. (Shakespeare's actors had to work in broad daylight.)*

[4]   Troilus   *He was separated from his beloved Cressida when she was taken from Troy to the camp of the besieging Greeks. A sequence of references to classic tales of unhappy love starts here. In such a game of 'swaps' Lorenzo and Jessica delight in their own, contrasted, happiness – without growing too 'moony' about it.*

[7]   Thisbe   *Tiptoeing over the dewy grass for a secret rendezvous with her lover Pyramus, she was frightened away by a lion whose shadow she saw in the moonlight. (Shakespeare makes a lot of fun of the whole sentimental story at the end of his play* A Midsummer Night's Dream.)

[10]   Dido   *The Queen of Carthage, abandoned by her lover, the wandering hero Aeneas. (The willow wand she waved became a symbol of forsaken love.)*

[13]   Medea   *An enchantress who helped Jason to win the golden fleece because she loved him. She restored his old father, Aeson, to youth. But for all her magic, Jason finally deserted her.*

[15]   steal from   *both 'desert' and 'rob'*

[16]   unthrift love   *both 'extravagant devotion' and 'impecunious lover'*

[19]   Stealing   *Taking up his teasing tone, she matches his charge of stealing (l. 15) with one of her own – giving the word a third sense of 'gaining possession of'.*

[21]   shrew   *scolding woman*

[22]   slander   *because she has implied that Lorenzo won't stay true to her.*

ACT FIVE

Scene 1. *Enter* LORENZO *and* JESSICA

LORENZO The moon shines bright. In such a night
    as this,
    When the sweet wind did gently kiss the trees
    And they did make no noise, in such a night
    Troilus methinks mounted the Troyan walls,
    And sighed his soul toward the Grecian tents
    Where Cressid lay that night.

JESSICA   In such a night
    Did Thisbe fearfully o'ertrip the dew,
    And saw the lion's shadow ere himself,
    And ran dismayed away.

LORENZO   In such a night
    Stood Dido with a willow in her hand   10
    Upon the wild sea banks, and waft her love
    To come again to Carthage.

JESSICA   In such a night
    Medea gathered the enchanted herbs
    That did renew old Aeson.

LORENZO   In such a night
    Did Jessica steal from the wealthy Jew,
    And with an unthrift love did run from Venice
    As far as Belmont.

JESSICA   In such a night
    Did young Lorenzo swear he loved her well,
    Stealing her soul with many vows of faith,
    And ne'er a true one.

LORENZO   In such a night   20
    Did pretty Jessica (like a little shrew)
    Slander her love, and he forgave it her.

[23] out-night you   *beat you at this game of 'in such a night'*

[25, 27] *It seems, from Lorenzo's questions, as though the night is darker now.*

[30–3] *The details of Stephano's message appropriately endorse the story that Portia told Lorenzo earlier (see III. 4. 26–32).*

[39] *As Lorenzo and Jessica begin to go in they are stopped by the arrival of Launcelot. He goes 'holloaing' around the stage, imitating the sound of the horn that a post-boy blows to announce his approach.*

[40–41] *compare ll. 25, 27*

[43–5] *Lorenzo and Jessica are probably standing mid-stage near one of the pillars which momentarily hides them from Launcelot's view.*

[47] horn full of good news   *The phrase suggests both the messenger's horn, announcing the good news, and a cornucopia (the horn of plenty, full of good things).*

JESSICA I would out-night you, did nobody come;
    But hark, I hear the footing of a man.

Enter STEPHANO, *a messenger*

LORENZO Who comes so fast in silence of the night?
STEPHANO A friend.
LORENZO A friend? What friend? Your name I pray
    you, friend?
STEPHANO Stephàno is my name, and I bring word
    My mistress will before the break of day
    Be here at Belmont. She doth stray about   30
    By holy crosses where she kneels and prays
    For happy wedlock hours.
LORENZO   Who comes with her?
STEPHANO None but a holy hermit and her maid.
    I pray you, is my master yet returned?
LORENZO He is not, nor we have not heard from him.
    But go we in, I pray thee, Jessica,
    And ceremoniously let us prepare
    Some welcome for the mistress of the house.

Enter LAUNCELOT GOBBO

LAUNCELOT Sola, sola! Wo ha ho! Sola, sola!
LORENZO Who calls?   40
LAUNCELOT Sola! Did you see Master Lorenzo?
    Master Lorenzo! Sola, sola!
LORENZO Leave holloaing, man! Here.
LAUNCELOT Sola! Where? Where?
LORENZO Here!
LAUNCELOT Tell him there's a post come from my
    master, with his horn full of good news. My
    master will be here ere morning.   [*Exit*

THE MERCHANT OF VENICE

[49] expect *await*

[50] *No doubt he changes his mind because the moon comes out again (l. 54).*
[51] signify *announce*

[55] *They probably sit at the foot of one of the pillars, the stage itself being 'this (grassy) bank'.*

[57] Become *suit*
    touches of *notes played in*
[58–9] *At this moment the actors are looking up at the real sky, while over their heads – in full view of the groundlings in the audience – is the 'floor' of the theatre's 'heaven' (see IV. 1. 185), richly decorated with stars and signs of the zodiac.*
[59] patens *Probably 'patterns' in Elizabethan spelling: possibly a version of 'patines' meaning 'small pieces of shining metal'.*
[60–2] *The Elizabethans believed that the stars, in their courses round the earth, were constantly producing different notes ('still quiring') which together made a heavenly harmony.*
[62] young-eyed cherubins *angels with very keen, ever-young eyesight*
[63–5] Such . . . hear it *Our human souls, being immortal like angels, are capable of appreciating the harmony in 'the music of the spheres', but while we live in the deadening, coarse dress of mortal flesh we cannot hear the actual music*

[Enter Musicians] *They probably play from the balcony above the inner stage.*
[66] Diana *moon-goddess and goddess of chastity. (A complimentary context in which to mention Portia.)*
[67] touches *see [57]*
[69] sweet *melodious (not necessarily happy)*
[70] The reason . . . attentive *That is because you respond so well to its influence*
[71] wanton *playful*
[72] race *breed*
    unhandled colts *young, untrained horses*

LORENZO Sweet soul, let's in, and there expect their
    coming.
    And yet no matter – why should we go in?   50
    My friend Stephàno, signify, I pray you,
    Within the house, your mistress is at hand,
    And bring your music forth into the air.
                    [*Exit* STEPHANO
    How sweet the moonlight sleeps upon this bank!
    Here will we sit and let the sounds of music
    Creep in our ears; soft stillness and the night
    Become the touches of sweet harmony.
    Sit, Jessica. Look how the floor of heaven
    Is thick inlaid with patens of bright gold.
    There's not the smallest orb which thou be-
        hold'st   60
    But in his motion like an angel sings,
    Still quiring to the young-eyed cherubins;
    Such harmony is in immortal souls,
    But whilst this muddy vesture of decay
    Doth grossly close it in, we cannot hear it.

Enter MUSICIANS

    Come ho, and wake Diana with a hymn.
    With sweetest touches pierce your mistress' ear
    And draw her home with music.

Music

JESSICA I am never merry when I hear sweet music.
LORENZO The reason is your spirits are attentive.   70
    For do but note a wild and wanton herd
    Or race of youthful and unhandled colts
    Fetching mad bounds, bellowing and neighing
        loud,

THE MERCHANT OF VENICE

[74] Which . . . blood *for it is their nature to behave so excitedly*

[77] make a mutual stand *all stand at the same time*
[78] modest *mild*
[79–80] the poet . . . floods *In Greek legend Orpheus was a musician whose playing attracted and charmed all natural things within earshot. His story is told by Ovid ('the poet') in his book* Metamorphoses *which, in translation, was a favourite piece of literature among the Elizabethans.*
[81] naught so stockish *there is nothing so insensitive*
[83–8] *A reminder that among humankind everything in the garden is not lovely. Shylock was precisely this kind of man, as the audience – if not the 'attentive' Jessica – may recall.*
[84] concord *harmony*
[85] fit for *capable of*
    stratagems and spoils *appalling plots and destructiveness*
[86] motions of his spirit *his instincts*
[87] affections *feelings*
    Erebus *one of the darkest regions on the way to Hell*

[89] *No doubt a candle-lantern hangs either in the inner stage or in the casement window above the door facing Portia and Nerissa. They 'approach' the house by walking slowly round the sides of the forestage during the next twenty lines.*
[91] naughty *wicked*

[94] substitute *deputy ruler*
[95–6] then . . . itself *his glory disappears (because the greater glory of the real king swamps it)*
[97] the main of waters *the ocean*

[99] Nothing . . . respect *Things are not good in themselves, but are made so by the circumstances in which we notice them*

Which is the hot condition of their blood,
If they but hear perchance a trumpet sound,
Or any air of music touch their ears,
You shall perceive them make a mutual stand,
Their savage eyes turned to a modest gaze
By the sweet power of music. Therefore the
   poet
Did feign that Orpheus drew trees, stones, and
   floods,   80
Since naught so stockish, hard, and full of rage
But music for the time doth change his nature.
The man that hath no music in himself,
Nor is not moved with concord of sweet sounds,
Is fit for treasons, stratagems, and spoils;
The motions of his spirit are dull as night,
And his affections dark as Erebus.
Let no such man be trusted. Mark the music.

Enter PORTIA *and* NERISSA

PORTIA That light we see is burning in my hall.
   How far that little candle throws his beams!   90
   So shines a good deed in a naughty world.
NERISSA When the moon shone we did not see the
   candle.
PORTIA So doth the greater glory dim the less.
   A substitute shines brightly as a king
   Until a king be by, and then his state
   Empties itself, as doth an inland brook
   Into the main of waters. Music, hark!
NERISSA It is your music, madam, of the house.
PORTIA Nothing is good, I see, without respect;
   Methinks it sounds much sweeter than by day.   100
NERISSA Silence bestows that virtue on it, madam.

THE MERCHANT OF VENICE

[103] attended *heeded*

[107–8] How many . . . perfection! *'What a lot of things are considered to be just right in their beauty and impressiveness ('seasoned') because one encounters them at just the right time ('season')!' By this time Portia and Nerissa have come up close to the lovers, who have not yet noticed them.*

[109] Endymion *Probably Portia's light-hearted comment on Lorenzo and Jessica in each other's arms. Endymion was a handsome young shepherd in Greek legend. The moon-goddess fell in love with him and kept him asleep for ever.*

[115] Which speed . . . words *and we hope they have benefited from our prayers*

[118] signify *announce*

[tucket] *a flourish on a trumpet*

[122] I hear his trumpet *Bassanio and Antonio have made better speed than Portia bargained for, it seems! (See IV. 1. 403 and IV. 2. 2–3.)*

PORTIA The crow doth sing as sweetly as the lark
When neither is attended; and I think
The nightingale, if she should sing by day
When every goose is cackling, would be thought
No better a musician than the wren.
How many things by season seasoned are
To their right praise and true perfection!
Peace, ho!

Music ceases

    The moon sleeps with Endymion,
And would not be awaked.

LORENZO   That is the voice,   110
Or I am much deceived, of Portia.

PORTIA [*To* NERISSA] He knows me as the blind man
    knows the cuckoo,
By the bad voice.

LORENZO   Dear lady, welcome home.

PORTIA We have been praying for our husbands'
    welfare,
Which speed we hope the better for our words.
Are they returned?

LORENZO   Madam, they are not yet,
But there is come a messenger before
To signify their coming.

PORTIA   Go in, Nerissa.
Give orders to my servants that they take
No note at all of our being absent hence –   120
Nor you, Lorenzo – Jessica, nor you.

A tucket sounds

LORENZO Your husband is at hand; I hear his
    trumpet.
We are no tell-tales, madam; fear you not.

[124] *Shakespeare begins to 'lighten' his scene – to 'season' (ll. 107–8) the arrival of the party from Venice, and to prepare the way for the imminent charade.*

[127–8] *Bassanio hears his wife's last words as he comes in, and in response to them tells her that she is radiant enough to make it daylight in Belmont when the sun is shining on the other side of the globe.*

[129–30] *To be a 'light' wife was to be an unfaithful one, to cuckold one's husband.*

[130] heavy   *miserable, wretched*

[132] God sort all!   *may all be as God wishes! (No doubt her coming 'quarrel' with Bassanio has crossed her mind!)*

[135] bound   *indebted*

[136] bound   *(in friendship)*

[137] bound   *(by Shylock's bond and by prison chains)*

[141] I scant this breathing courtesy   *I cut short this welcome which is only spoken*

[142] *Clearly Gratiano has returned not to a welcome but to a sharp (mimed) rebuke during the last fifteen lines.*

[144] Would he were gelt   *I wish he' had been castrated*
      for my part   *I must say*

[148] posy   *inscription (inside the ring). Mottoes were often inscribed on cheap knives also, in rhyme (po-e-sy), as a sales gimmick.*

PORTIA This night methinks is but the daylight sick;
    It looks a little paler. 'Tis a day
    Such as the day is when the sun is hid.

Enter BASSANIO, ANTONIO, GRATIANO *and their*
followers

BASSANIO We should hold day with the Antipodes,
    If you would walk in absence of the sun.
PORTIA Let me give light, but let me not be light,
    For a light wife doth make a heavy husband,   130
    And never be Bassanio so for me.
    But God sort all! You are welcome home, my
      lord.
BASSANIO I thank you, madam. Give welcome to my
      friend.
    This is the man, this is Antonio,
    To whom I am so infinitely bound.
PORTIA You should in all sense be much bound to
      him,
    For, as I hear, he was much bound for you.
ANTONIO No more than I am well acquitted of.
PORTIA Sir, you are very welcome to our house.
    It must appear in other ways than words,   140
    Therefore I scant this breathing courtesy.
GRATIANO [*To* NERISSA] By yonder moon I swear
      you do me wrong!
    In faith, I gave it to the judge's clerk.
    Would he were gelt that had it, for my part,
    Since you do take it, love, so much at heart.
PORTIA A quarrel ho, already! What's the matter?
GRATIANO About a hoop of gold, a paltry ring
    That she did give me, whose posy was

[150] leave me not   both 'don't desert Nerissa' and 'don't part
with this ring'
[151] What   why
[152] compare IV. 2. 14

[155] for   for the sake of

[156] respective   careful and respectful (of your own honour)

[159] an if he live   so long as he lives

[162] scrubbèd   stunted

[164] prating   talkative

[172] leave   part with
[173-4] the wealth . . . masters   all the money in the world

[175] unkind   both 'cruel' and 'unnatural'
        grief   grievance
[176] And 'twere to me   if I were treated so

      For all the world like cutler's poetry
      Upon a knife, 'Love me, and leave me not.'   150
NERISSA What talk you of the posy or the value?
      You swore to me when I did give it you
      That you would wear it till your hour of death,
      And that it should lie with you in your grave.
      Though not for me, yet for your vehement
         oaths,
      You should have been respective and have kept
         it.
      Gave it a judge's clerk! No, God's my judge,
      The clerk will ne'er wear hair on's face that had
         it!
GRATIANO He will, an if he live to be a man.
NERISSA Ay, if a woman live to be a man.   160
GRATIANO Now by this hand, I gave it to a youth,
      A kind of boy, a little scrubbèd boy
      No higher than thyself, the judge's clerk,
      A prating boy that begged it as a fee.
      I could not for my heart deny it him.
PORTIA You were to blame – I must be plain with
         you –
      To part so slightly with your wife's first gift,
      A thing stuck on with oaths upon your
         finger
      And so riveted with faith unto your flesh.
      I gave my love a ring, and made him swear   170
      Never to part with it; and here he stands.
      I dare be sworn for him he would not leave it,
      Nor pluck it from his finger, for the wealth
      That the world masters. Now in faith, Gratiano,
      You give your wife too unkind a cause of grief.
      And 'twere to me, I should be mad at it.

[190–2] *The 'partnership' of the two wives in their practical joke on their husbands is emphasised on the stage by Nerissa's 'echoing' of not only the words of Portia (ll. 234, 260) but also her gestures and actions of feigned anger, from this point until the truth is revealed.*

[193–202] *The verbal repetition stresses the dramatic point – Bassanio cannot avoid his fault with 'the ring', try as he may to excuse himself.*

[198] You would ... displeasure *you would stop being so cross. (Bassanio's oddly formal turn of phrase here indicates the strength of his discomfiture.)*

[199] virtue *power, strength (as a token of love)*

[201] Or your ... ring *or how much it was your duty (as my husband) to keep the ring*

BASSANIO [*Aside*] Why, I were best to cut my left
    hand off
    And swear I lost the ring defending it.

GRATIANO My Lord Bassanio gave his ring away
    Unto the judge that begged it, and indeed   180
    Deserved it too; and then the boy, his clerk
    That took some pains in writing, he begged
      mine;
    And neither man nor master would take aught
    But the two rings.

PORTIA   What ring gave you, my lord?
    Not that, I hope, which you received of me.

BASSANIO If I could add a lie unto a fault,
    I would deny it; but you see my finger
    Hath not the ring upon it – it is gone.

PORTIA Even so void is your false heart of truth!
    By heaven, I will ne'er come in your bed   190
    Until I see the ring.

NERISSA [*To* GRATIANO]   Nor I in yours
    Till I again see mine!

BASSANIO   Sweet Portia,
    If you did know to whom I gave the ring,
    If you did know for whom I gave the ring,
    And would conceive for what I gave the ring,
    And how unwillingly I left the ring
    When nought would be accepted but the ring,
    You would abate the strength of your dis-
      pleasure.

PORTIA If you had known the virtue of the ring,
    Or half her worthiness that gave the ring,   200
    Or your own honour to contain the ring,
    You would not then have parted with the ring.
    What man is there so much unreasonable,

THE MERCHANT OF VENICE

[205] With any terms of zeal   *at all vigorously*
[205–6] wanted . . . ceremony   *who would be so lacking in tact
as to press you to give up something you held sacred.* (*Antonio was such
a man!*)

[210] a civil doctor   *both 'a doctor of civil law' and 'a courteous
doctor'*

[213] suffered him to   *let him*

[216] I was enforced to   *I had no choice but to*
[217] beset with   *overcome by a sense of*

[221] Had you   *if you had*

[226] liberal   *free and easy in giving things away*

[229] Know him I shall   *both 'I shall recognise him' and 'I
will certainly sleep with him'*
[230] Argus   *In Greek myth this creature had a hundred eyes
of which only two were asleep at any one time. He was thus an ideal
watchman.*

If you had pleased to have defended it
With any terms of zeal, wanted the modesty
To urge the thing held as a ceremony?
Nerissa teaches me what to believe –
I'll die for't but some woman had the ring!
BASSANIO No, by my honour, madam! By my soul
No woman had it, but a civil doctor,   210
Which did refuse three thousand ducats of me
And begged the ring, the which I did deny him,
And suffered him to go displeased away –
Even he that had held up the very life
Of my dear friend. What should I say, sweet
    lady?
I was enforced to send it after him.
I was beset with shame and courtesy.
My honour would not let ingratitude
So much besmear it. Pardon me, good lady!
For by these blessèd candles of the night,   220
Had you been there, I think you would have
    begged
The ring of me to give the worthy doctor.
PORTIA Let not that doctor e'er come near my house.
Since he hath got the jewel that I loved,
And that which you did swear to keep for me,
I will become as liberal as you;
I'll not deny him anything I have –
No, not my body nor my husband's bed.
Know him I shall, I am well sure of it.
Lie not a night from home. Watch me like
    Argus –   230
If you do not, if I be left alone,
Now by mine honour which is yet mine own,
I'll have that doctor for my bedfellow.

[234] be well advised   *take good care*

[235] to mine own protection   *to take care of my own honour*

[236] take him   *catch him (at it)*

[237] I'll mar . . . pen   *I'll spoil both his professional and his sexual equipment*

[238] I am the unhappy subject of   *I'm afraid I am responsible for*

[240] enforcèd wrong   *see* [216]

[244] In both . . . himself   *in looking into my eyes he sees his reflection twice*

[245] double   *both 'two-fold' and 'false'*

[246] oath of credit   *an oath worth believing (I must say!)*

[249] for his wealth   *to bring him happiness*

[251] Had quite miscarried   *had been altogether lost*

[253] advisedly   *deliberately*

NERISSA [*To* GRATIANO] And I his clerk. Therefore
    be well advised
    How you do leave me to mine own protection.
GRATIANO Well, do you so. Let not me take him
    then;
    For if I do, I'll mar the young clerk's pen!
ANTONIO I am th'unhappy subject of these quarrels.
PORTIA Sir, grieve not you – you are welcome not-
    withstanding.
BASSANIO Portia, forgive me this enforcèd wrong,   240
    And in the hearing of these many friends
    I swear to thee, even by thine own fair eyes
    Wherein I see myself—
PORTIA [*To* NERISSA]   Mark you but that!
    In both my eyes he doubly sees himself;
    In each eye one. [*To* BASSANIO] Swear by your
    double self,
    And there's an oath of credit.
BASSANIO   Nay, but hear me.
    Pardon this fault, and by my soul I swear
    I never more will break an oath with thee.
ANTONIO I once did lend my body for his wealth,
    Which but for him that had your husband's ring 250
    Had quite miscarried. I dare be bound again,
    My soul upon the forfeit, that your lord
    Will never more break faith advisedly.
PORTIA Then you shall be his surety.

            She gives ANTONIO *her ring*

                      Give him this,
    And bid him keep it better than the other.
ANTONIO Here, Lord Bassanio. Swear to keep this
    ring.

THE MERCHANT OF VENICE

[258] of *from*

[259] lay with *slept with*

[262] In lieu of *in return for*

[263–5] *Just as roads should not need mending in summer when fair weather keeps them in good condition, so wives should not need to take lovers to bed when they have new and faithful husbands only too ready to satisfy them.*

[265] cuckolds . . . deserved it? *husbands whose wives have been unfaithful to us before we have had a chance to show them how good we are in bed? (The marriages of Bassanio and Gratiano are still unconsummated; see III. 2. 310–12.)*

[266] Speak not so grossly *Don't be so coarse.*

 all amazed *thoroughly bewildered*

[276] argosies *large merchant ships*

[276–9] *Shakespeare's short cut to a restoration of Antonio's fortunes is rather more convincing on the stage than on the page!*

[281] Were you . . . cuckold *see ll. 234–5*

[283] Unless . . . man *compare ll. 159–60*

BASSANIO By heaven, it is the same I gave the doctor!
PORTIA I had it of him. Pardon me, Bassanio,
For by this ring the doctor lay with me.
NERISSA And pardon me, my gentle Gratiano,   260
For that same scrubbèd boy, the doctor's clerk,

She gives GRATIANO *her ring*

In lieu of this last night did lie with me.
GRATIANO Why, this is like the mending of high-
ways
In summer, where the ways are fair enough!
What, are we cuckolds ere we have deserved it?
PORTIA Speak not so grossly. You are all amazed.
Here is a letter; read it at your leisure.
It comes from Padua from Bellario.
There you shall find that Portia was the doctor,
Nerissa there her clerk. Lorenzo here   270
Shall witness I set forth as soon as you
And even but now returned. I have not yet
Entered my house. Antonio, you are welcome,
And I have better news in store for you
Than you expect. Unseal this letter soon;
There you shall find three of your argosies
Are richly come to harbour suddenly.
You shall not know by what strange accident
I chancèd on this letter.
ANTONIO   I am dumb!
BASSANIO [*To* PORTIA] Were you the doctor, and I
knew you not?   280
GRATIANO [*To* NERISSA] Were you the clerk that is to
make me cuckold?
NERISSA Ay, but the clerk that never means to do it,
Unless he live until he be a man.

[286] life and living   *She saved his life in Venice, and here in Belmont she has given him something to live* on.

[288] road   *anchorage*

[294] manna   *life-saving food (which the Israelites found in the wilderness and believed to be a gift from Heaven)*

[296–7] you are not . . . at full   *you are not really clear in your minds about the way these things have come to pass*
[298] And . . . inter'gatories   *and (like witnesses in a court of law) we will be called on to answer a whole series of questions on oath*

[305] couching   *going to bed*
[306–7] Well . . . ring   *Well, as long as I live nothing will be as important to me as (i) looking after the ring Nerissa has given me and (ii) ensuring that I am the only one who makes love to her!*

BASSANIO [*To* PORTIA] Sweet doctor, you shall be my
    bedfellow.
    When I am absent, then lie with my wife.

ANTONIO Sweet lady, you have given me life and
    living;
    For here I read for certain that my ships
    Are safely come to road.

PORTIA   How now, Lorenzo?
    My clerk hath some good comforts too for you.

NERISSA Ay, and I'll give them him without a fee.   290
    There do I give to you and Jessica
    From the rich Jew, a special deed of gift,
    After his death, of all he dies possessed of.

LORENZO Fair ladies, you drop manna in the way
    Of starvèd people.

PORTIA   It is almost morning,
    And yet I am sure you are not satisfied
    Of these events at full. Let us go in,
    And charge us there upon inter'gatories,
    And we will answer all things faithfully.

GRATIANO Let it be so. The first inter'gatory   300
    That my Nerissa shall be sworn on is
    Whether till the next night she had rather stay,
    Or go to bed now, being two hours to day.
    But were the day come, I should wish it dark
    Till I were couching with the doctor's clerk.
    Well, while I live I'll fear no other thing
    So sore, as keeping safe Nerissa's ring.

                            [*Exeunt*

Also produced by Macmillan
Shakespeare Interviews

devised, written and directed by Robert Tanitch

Four tapes, each of which contains a brief introduction to
one of Shakespeare's most popular plays, followed by a
searching interview with the main characters in the play.
The actions and motives of the characters, and the conflict
and drama of their relationships are revealed through the
interviewer's skilful questioning.

 Shakespeare Interviews can be enjoyed both at a simple
and a sophisticated level. For the student coming to
Shakespeare for the first time, these tapes will be invaluable
in helping him to overcome the initial language barrier.
For the student of Shakespeare at CSE, O and A level who
is familiar with the play which he is studying, these tapes
offer a stimulating approach, and a springboard for new
ideas.

Characters interviewed:
Macbeth: Macbeth, Lady Macbeth
Julius Caesar: Brutus, Cassius, Julius Caesar, Mark Antony
Hamlet: Hamlet, Ophelia, Polonius, Claudius, Gertrude
Romeo and Juliet: Romeo, Juliet, Mercutio, Friar Lawrence,
the Nurse

Macbeth	open reel 333 15111 9	cassette 333 15373 1
Julius Caesar	open reel 333 15112 7	cassette 333 15375 8
Hamlet	open reel 333 15113 5	cassette 333 15376 6
Romeo and		
Juliet	open reel 333 15114 3	cassette 333 15377 4